CASE STUDIES IN
CULTURAL ANTHROPOLOGY

SERIES EDITORS

George and Louise Spindler

STANFORD UNIVERSITY

SIMBU LAW

Conflict Management in the
New Guinea Highlands

SIMBU LAW

Conflict Management in
the New Guinea Highlands

AARON PODOLEFSKY

Dean
College of Social and Behavioral Sciences
University of Northern Iowa

HARCOURT BRACE JOVANOVICH COLLEGE PUBLISHERS

FORT WORTH   PHILADELPHIA   SAN DIEGO   NEW YORK
ORLANDO   AUSTIN   SAN ANTONIO   TORONTO
MONTREAL   LONDON   SYNDEY   TOKYO

Publisher: Ted Buchholz
Acquisitions Editor: Chris Klein
Project Editor: Steve Norder
Production Manager: Jane Tyndall Ponceti
Book Designer: Sue Hart

Printed in the United States of America

Library of Congress Cataloging-in-Publication Data

Podolefsky, Aaron.
   Simbu law : conflict management in the New Guinea highlands /
Aaron Podolefsky.
      p.   cm. — (Case studies in cultural anthropology)
   Includes bibliographical references and index.
   ISBN 0-03-073329-4
   1. Chimbu (Papua New Guinea people)—Mediation. 2. Chimbu (Papua
New Guinea people)—Social conditions. 3. Dispute resolution (Law)-
-Papua New Guinea—Chimbu Province. 4. Mediation—Papua New Guinea-
-Chimbu Province. 5. Conflict management—Papua New Guinea—Chimbu
Province. 6. Chimbu Province (Papua New Guinea)—Social conditions.
   I. Title. II. Series.
   DU740.42.P63   1992
   303.6'9'0899912—dc20   91-46906
                                                                  CIP

0-03-073329-4

2 3 4 5 6 7 8 9 0 1   016   9 8 7 6 5 4 3 2 1

Dedicated to my grandparents

Sylvia and Sigmund Horowitz

Ida and Solomon Podolefsky

Lillian (Lotta) and Morris Tamres

Foreword

ABOUT THE SERIES

These case studies in cultural anthropology are designed for students in beginning and intermediate courses in the social sciences, to bring them insights into the richness and complexity of human life as it is lived in different ways, in different places. The authors are men and women who have lived in the societies they write about and who are professionally trained as observers and interpreters of human behavior. Also, the authors are teachers; in their writing, the needs of the student reader remain foremost. It is our belief that when an understanding of ways of life very different from one's own is gained, abstractions and generalizations about the human condition become meaningful.

The scope and character of the series have changed constantly since we published the first case studies in 1960, in keeping with our intention to represent anthropology as it is. We are concerned with the ways in which human groups and communities are coping with the massive changes wrought in their physical and sociopolitical environments in recent decades. We are also concerned with the ways in which established cultures have solved life's problems. And we want to include representation of the various modes of communication and emphasis that are being formed and reformed as anthropology itself changes.

We think of this series as an instructional series, intended for use in the classroom. We, the editors, have always used case studies in our teaching, whether for beginning students or advanced graduate students. We start with case studies, drawn from our own series or elsewhere, weave our way into theory, and then turn again to cases. For us, they are the grounding of our discipline.

ABOUT THE AUTHOR

Aaron Podolefsky was born on June 20, 1946, in Los Angeles, California. His early years were spent commuting between New York City and the San Francisco Bay Area. He graduated from Mountain View High School in 1964 and went on to California State University at San Jose, where he earned a degree in Mathematics in 1968. He began his teaching career as a mathematics teacher in New York. In an effort to broaden his education, he enrolled in an evening program leading to a master's degree in liberal studies at the State University of New York at Stony Brook. A few courses in anthropology led to a dramatic turn-around in his life's goals. In 1973 he began serious graduate study in anthropology. In that same year he married Ronnie Shapiro, who shared with him the trials of graduate school and of life in the New Guinea Highlands. Following the completion of his master's degree and doctorate from Stony Brook, he accepted a research associate position at Northwestern University's Center for Urban Affairs and Policy Research, where he investigated collective responses to crime in urban America. Dr. Podolefsky has authored books on community crime prevention and edited texts on applying anthropology to contemporary human problems. During his career, Dr. Podolefsky has served on the faculty at West Virginia University and chaired the Department of Sociology, Anthropology and Social Work at Western Kentucky University. He is presently dean of the College of Social and Behavioral Sciences at the University of Northern Iowa.

ABOUT THIS CASE STUDY

Conflict is a universal experience in human society. In all societies, large or small, traditional or modern, rich or poor, people disagree over values, fight over property, or are injured in ways real or imaginary. Some societies have developed legal systems with judges, juries, and correctional institutions, other societies have not. One might wonder how order is maintained in societies lacking judges with the authority to decide cases and impose penalties. Are these "lawless" societies inevitably characterized by violence and brutality?

The original intent in the construction of the Case Studies in Cultural Anthropology series was to provide well-rounded, readable descriptive analyses of distinctive cultures for introductory and intermediate courses in anthropology. This remains a basic purpose of the series but with the increasing specialization of our discipline, recent case studies have become more focused on certain aspects of sociocultural structure and process. Chagnon's *Yanomamo* and Keiser's *Kohistani (Friends by Day and Enemy by Night)* provide examples of how some human communities attempt to resolve conflicts and settle disputes through violence or the threat of violence. *Simbu Law* provides an interesting complement because, although warfare and violence are common in the New Guinea Highlands, its focus is on conflict management through mediation. Even though there are no formal courts, no magistrates, no police, no chiefs, and no centralized authority, there is settlement of disputes and conflict resolution.

The *Simbu*, a New Guinea Highland people, live in an *acephelous* society, meaning literally "without a head." With tribal groupings of about four thousand people and a local population density of 270 persons per square mile, the *Simbu* would seem to require governance by some form of centralized authority. Such authority now exists, albeit somewhat loosely applied, through the new republic and recently colonial governments. No such authority existed before the recent present and the traditional structure and process of dispute settlement persist despite recent changes in governance.

It is this traditional process of conflict management that Aaron Podolefsky has studied in his fieldwork with the *Simbu*. As an anthropologist should, he was "on the spot" when the conflicts occurred, and followed, as an eyewitness, the processes of settlement. He provides the reader with sixy-five cases, quoting the principle actors at length and describing the details of the procedures involved in settlements. He also uses government records and memory cases, in addition to the observed cases.

The case approach is well established in common law. Case materials provide information on rules and sanctions as well as on settlement and resolution and in general document the legal process.

The processes of conflict resolution display the culture at work and are one key to understanding any culture. For these reasons *Simbu Law* tells us much about Simbu culture as well as about conflict resolution and dispute settlement in an acephelous society, a type of sociopolitical structure that is widespread, even in the modernizing world of today.

George and Louise Spindler
Series Editors
Ethnographics
P.O. Box 38
Calistoga, CA, 94515

Acknowledgments

I was first introduced to the Simbu by Professor Paula Brown, who guided my graduate study and who has remained a friend and mentor over many many years. Professor June Starr first stimulated my interest in anthropology and guided me through the literature on the anthropological study of law. Richard Scaglion read an earlier draft of this manuscript and made numerous helpful suggestions, as did a number of anonymous reviewers.

Field research among the Simbu was funded by a grant from the National Science Foundation, which is gratefully acknowledged.

It is impossible to express my debt to the Simbu people themselves. To the many individuals who took me, my wife, and my son into their lives and forever changed ours, thank you.

Contents

CASES

MEMORY CASES

OBSERVED CASES

FIGURES

TABLES

ILLUSTRATIONS

Introduction

Acephelous society constitutes the oldest form of human social organiza-
tion and the only one that defines and responds to troublesome behavior
without some form of centralized political power.

Raymond J. Michalowski, 1985

Western scholars have long been fascinated by the customs and manners of people from other cultures. How do they organize their social lives, provide food and shelter, and maintain order? During the Enlightenment, social philosophers believed humans once lived in a "state of nature." Some, like the French philosopher Jean Jacques Rousseau, imagined a world with no conflict; small bands gathered food from nature's bounty and shared the products of their labor. Rousseau envisioned the noble savage living in harmony without the need of centralized government, class distinctions, private property, or formalized religion. He wrote, in 1754, "There is hardly any inequality among men in the state of nature." More adventurous spirits, such as Thomas Hobbes, who wrote *Leviathan* in 1651, imagined the state of nature as a war of all against all. Without external controls, our innately nasty and brutish human nature emerged; in the absence of centralized governments and formal religion, conflict was pervasive.

Because we are social animals, the question of order is fundamental to understanding ourselves and our social arrangements. Most of us are raised in the Hobbesian tradition; we believe that humans will get away with whatever they can unless external controls keep us from following our natural instincts. To us in Western society the problem of maintaining order falls to the study of law and legal systems.

During the 1960s, when I was an undergraduate, questions about human nature were a frequent topic of conversation among students. With the war in Vietnam raging and the civil rights movement in full swing, university students raised fundamental questions about society, human nature, and social conflict—many of today's students have the same thirst for knowledge. While friends and I debated these issues late into the night, I had little opportunity, as an undergraduate majoring in mathematics, to study such things formally. A few years after I graduated I decided to round out my education by pursuing a master's degree in liberal studies.

I'll never forget how I got into my first anthropology course. The class was full, and I decided to see the professor about the possibility of getting in. I found him walking across the lawn, and as we walked I expressed my fascination with Robert Ardry's book *African Genesis*. Though the topic was anthropological, the author

1

was not an anthropologist and the book had not garnered great respect among scholars. I can only imagine what the professor was thinking, but he let me in the course—probably to give me a taste of "real" anthropology.

I learned, to my surprise, that there are societies that have no police, no courts, and no jails. I suppose that if someone had really pressed me on the question I would have known, even before studying anthropology, that some societies have no jails. Certainly the Eskimo have none, and I could see why they wouldn't need any. But until taking anthropology I had never thought about the real possibility of a society without prisons. Neither had I given much thought to the possibility of a society without judges or police of some kind, however informally recognized. For me, the idea of a society lacking police, courts, and correctional facilities had the mythlike qualities of utopian novels or social philosophy.

Some societies, I learned, even lack chiefs who can command a following or order a fine or punishment. Such societies are called *acephelous,* meaning "without a head." Acephelous societies lack identifiable rulers with the power to direct or command other members of the society.

This certainly is not the way tribal societies are treated in the fiction media, and nothing in my four years of college, majoring in mathematics, had made me aware of the dazzling diversity of social arrangements found across our ever shrinking planet. As my interest in the anthropological study of law developed, I learned of the people who live in the high mountains of New Guinea.

New Guinea is the second largest island in the world. With 183,000 square miles, the island approximates the combined size of the states of Illinois, Indiana, Ohio, Kentucky, Tennessee, and West Virginia. Although it lies just six degrees south of the equator, snow falls on the 14,000-foot mountain peaks and frosts are common above 10,000 feet.

This vast, unexplored island was divided among several colonial powers during the last part of the nineteenth century. The Dutch claimed the western half, while the eastern half was further divided, with the Germans taking the north and the British claiming the south. West New Guinea remained under Dutch colonial rule until 1963, when control was turned over to Indonesia under the name of West Irian. In 1906 the newly formed Commonwealth of Australia took over the administration of British New Guinea, changing the name to Papua. In 1914, a few days after the beginning of World War I, Australia seized control of the German area, which they maintained under military administration for the next seven years. The League of Nations gave Australia a mandate to govern the formerly German area in 1921. Thus, Australia controlled Papua in the south and New Guinea in the north, claiming them as a colony until Papua New Guinea became independent in 1975.

The clearest dichotomy in Papua New Guinea was (and still is) between the coastal region and the interior. The coastal people had been in contact with Europeans since the days of Captain Cook, when the nations of the West mapped, charted, and began to colonize much of the Pacific. But the interior was different— very different.

The center of this far-away, mysterious island was an enigma. Ringed by deadly, malaria-infested swampland just inland from a range of coastal mountains,

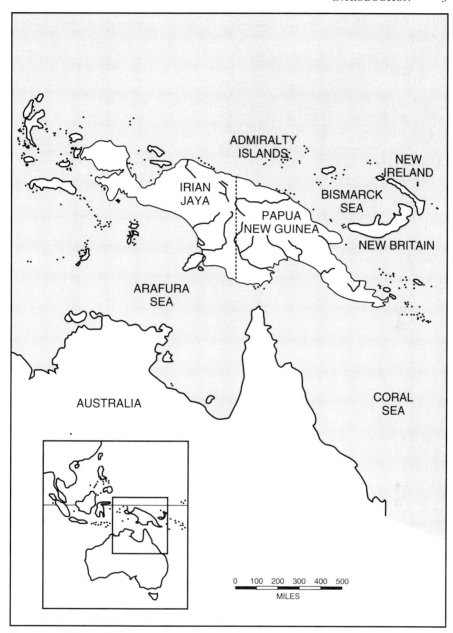

Location of New Guinea

the unexplored interior was thought to be uninhabited and remained isolated from the outside world until the early 1930s. Then, driven by the lust for gold, prospectors forged inland, discovering what was the last large population unknown to the Western world. Some gold was found, which caused something of a gold rush. But exploration was slow over the tortuous terrain.[1] World War II interrupted efforts to chart the interior, so the earliest anthropological investigation did not begin until the 1950s. Most people had only occasional contact, such as when a government patrol walked through their area asking people to register for the census. The farther from the central town of each Highland province, the less contact.

Between a million and a million and a half people, representing thousands of tribal groups and speaking hundreds of different languages, now live with one foot in the Stone Age and the other in the modern world. Change is coming extremely quickly, but tradition persists. Men and women continue to live separately, pigs are raised to be given away, and tribal warfare using featherless arrows and black palm wood spears remains a major problem into the 1990s.

Papua New Guinea has in fact provided a "window of opportunity" to enhance the understanding of culture and society by allowing the observation of cultures that have only recently been influenced by modern society. While we may no longer call these cultures pristine, I would argue that fundamental social institutions, like leadership, change less than more obvious and superficial traits, like styles of dress. Although there are elected councilors, as discussed in chapter 2, their influence over events and decisions, as in dispute cases, remains strongly imbedded in the local community. As government-backed police, courts, and corrections reach further into the bush, however, the window through which we may examine traditional law begins to close. At the same time, other new and possibly even more exciting questions emerge, such as the role of customary law in the development of a national legal system. But the fundamental questions need to be addressed first. How do New Guinea Highlanders resolve conflict, and what is the role of leaders in this process?

These recently discovered cultures do not have chiefs. While scholars disagree over how much authority traditional leaders held, most characterize these societies as acephelous. This seemed the perfect area to pursue my interest in how people resolve troubles in a society lacking a formal, institutionalized legal system. And so, toward the end of 1976, my wife, year-old son, and I found ourselves packing our bags for what promised to be the most exciting adventure of our lives—anthropological fieldwork among the Simbu of the Papua New Guinea Highlands. Our expectations were fulfilled, and we returned somewhat worse for wear but wiser for the experience.

Although they do not have chiefs or formal legal mechanisms, the Simbu are no small band of hunters and gatherers. They are densely populated agriculturalists who own land individually, passing ownership rights from father to son, generation after generation. The tribal societies of the New Guinea Highlands, including the Simbu, are known for the frequency and intensity of their warfare. Researchers have written far less about law or mechanisms for resolving conflict within tribes. The reasons for this include the inaccessibility of the island's vast interior, the lack

At home in our grass-walled house, the author rewrites fieldnotes on the day's events.

of research done before the 1950s, and the absence of apparent judicial institutions. It is very difficult to study "law" if there are no police or courts or anything else that looks like the legal apparatus we are used to. While scholars argued over the definition of law, the study of what people did in conflict situations sometimes slipped past us.

Since 1965, thanks to the suggestions of Laura Nader in America and A. L. Epstein in Britain, anthropologists spend less time trying to define law and more time studying the behavior of people struggling to resolve conflicts.

There are at least three reasons why we should focus on conflict behavior, rather than getting hung up over the definition of law. First, we want to understand how people in societies like the Simbu handle conflict. Without case studies such as this we cannot compare the range of ways humans deal with conflict, and without such comparisons we may come to believe that our way of handling conflict (or arranging marriages or praying to God) is the only and natural way for humans to do it. In a wider sense, therefore, anthropology calls on us to explore the diversity of the human condition.

The second reason is that studies of societies like the Simbu reveal that people who live in close-knit communities emphasize resolving conflict rather than going to court and winning. There are good reasons for this, which we in America have apparently forgotten. During the last two decades scholars and policy makers became aware that the American judicial system is inappropriate in cases between relatives, neighbors, friends, or others who are long-term, valued acquaintances because it fails to help them get to the root of the problem. Rather than coming to an agreement, courtroom dramas often escalate, people leaving more angry than they arrived. In response, we have been experimenting with a variety of alternatives to adjudication. The Ohio Night Prosecutor's Program, the San Francisco Community Boards, and other Neighborhood Justice Centers have been established to help citizens resolve minor disputes. An American Friends Service publication, *The Citizens' Dispute Resolution Handbook,* mentions that it was an anthropologist's description of conflict management in Africa that stimulated their work in local-level dispute resolution.

Conflict management research provides insights that are applicable to various types of dispute or geographical locale. For example, Jacob Bercovitch, in his book *Social Conflicts and Third Parties,* provides chapters on interpersonal conflict, labor-management conflict, and international conflict. Similarly, Roger Fisher and William Ury's *Getting to Yes* describes techniques of "principled negotiation" that can be applied to many types of conflict.

One feature many conflict situations have in common is that, for one reason or another, adjudication by an official with the authority to impose a decision is either inappropriate or unavailable. In the international arena, for example, no third-party nation has authority over another sovereign state. In the arena of marital conflicts or disputes between neighbors, adjudication leads to outcomes that are binding but do not necessarily resolve the source of the disagreement.

This is the third reason that case studies of societies like this are important. The absence of an authoritarian third party is a primary characteristic of acephelous society. In traditional New Guinea societies, as in the international arena, no legitimate authority for making adjudicatory decisions exists. By studying one New Guinea Highlands society, the Simbu, we can see how people deal with public conflict in the absence of authoritarian figures. This may generate theories of conflict resolution that can be applied in many settings.

Today, acephelous societies, such as the Simbu, exist within larger national political systems that have police, courts, and jails—but nearly all conflict occurs within a community of kin and neighbors. While adjudication is available, it may not be appropriate or convenient, and people choose not to use it. The anthropological study of small-scale acephelous societies can help us understand the fundamental processes of managing conflict.

We study anthropology to learn about other cultures, to reflect on and improve our own society, and to develop our understanding of social and cultural processes at a more abstract or theoretical level. Anthropology is a mirror calling us to reflect on our own ways of doing things. We study others to help see ourselves more clearly. Through self-examination, we may gain insights that will help improve our own country.

This book, in the anthropological tradition, is a case study of conflict management within a particular society. I made the assumption that people come into conflict in all societies and set out to discover the variety of ways individuals choose to deal with it. Set within the larger context of culture and social relations, I explore the range of options and how people decide to remedy the situation.

The goal of this book is to understand the disputing process. To do this I find it necessary to work at two levels: at the macro level of social institutions and at the micro level of individual behaviors. In the first two chapters I examine the concept of law and describe those aspects of Simbu society that are relevant to this study. Chapters 3 through 5 describe the alternatives available for handling conflict and present a number of actual dispute cases recorded in the field. Chapter 6 provides an analysis of the criteria used by individuals to make decisions about disputing strategies. The final chapter examines how the structure of society and the history of relations between people and groups influence individuals' goals, the interaction during a dispute, and the outcome.

Conflict and conflict management have always been with us. But, to borrow a phrase from Fisher and Ury, conflict is a growth industry. As the world shrinks, as people from different cultural backgrounds come into more frequent contact, and as people live in increasingly crowded conditions, we will need to place greater emphasis on resolving conflicts rather than on winning battles. Let me now tell you about the Simbu and how they preserve order in their society.

Note

1. The period is wonderfully documented in the film *First Contact,* which combines original black-and-white footage with recent interviews of New Guinea Highlanders and Australians who experienced this historic moment firsthand.

1 / Law and the Disputing Process

The morning began like any other in the New Guinea Highlands. The sweet smell of fresh, crisp air after a long night's rain, exotic birds singing songs of the forest, and roosters welcoming the morning sun. At the door of my two-room, grass-walled house, I welcomed the day, looking out over the horizon where the deep-blue equatorial sky met the lush green of the mountain forests. The intensity of color mirrored the depth of feeling that came with each new day in the field. Usually the day crept up slowly, but this one began with a bang.

It was April 15, 1977, and on this day two elderly men, Sine and Gui, walked two hours down the steep and winding mountain path from the hamlet of Baune to Mul. Along the way they chopped down two small trees and made a pair of 3-inch-thick fighting staffs. When they reached Mul, they moved quickly across the ceremonial ground toward an old man named Sago, who sat cross-legged on the ground. Before anyone knew what was happening, Sine and Gui attacked old Sago.

I was sitting drinking my morning coffee when the commotion erupted. I grabbed my field bag, which I kept packed with notebooks, cassette recorder, and camera, slung it over my shoulder, and dashed off to the ceremonial ground forty yards away. I found the three men circling one another. Although each had a steel axe tucked in his belt, none drew the lethal weapon. As Sago attempted to parry one blow after another, the air filled with the shouts of kin and neighbors rushing to see what was happening. Adrenalin pumped furiously through my veins, for I had little idea what might happen next. I knew how easily violence can expand into confrontations between larger and larger groups. At last, a few men separated Sine, Gui, and Sago, and relative calm settled over the scene.

Because the fighting ended before any serious injuries occurred, the men would attempt to settle the dispute within the community. As the dust settled, I wondered what had led to such an act of violence, what other options had been open to the men, why had they chosen this particular strategy, what would happen next, and what the final outcome would be.

Questions such as these brought me to the Papua New Guinea Highlands and are the focus of this book. Throughout graduate school I had been fascinated by the paradoxical question of law in New Guinea. The high population density and individual ownership of land found in some areas highlight the need for law, but the lack of chiefs, authoritarian offices, and clear social hierarchies suggest the absence of law, as some might define it. The stateless societies of New Guinea lack identifiable rulers endowed with the authority to command others or to make

9

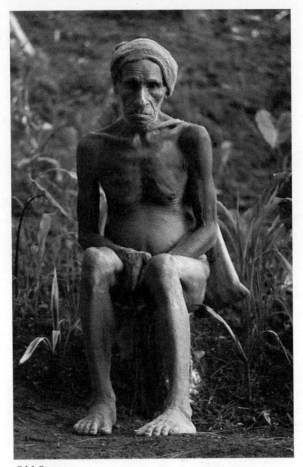

Old Sago

judicial decisions. Thus, according to most definitions, they lack "law." And, as Raymond Michalowski (1985:45) notes, "For many Americans *law* and *order* are inseparable, and there is a tendency to assume that societies without any formal legal system are probably characterized by violence, brutality, chaos, and theft."

I was struck by the inherent contradiction of a society without order. There is no doubt that people come into conflict, and there must be, I felt, ways for people to handle grievances without resorting to violence.

I begin this study with the assumption that conflicts and disputes exist and are a fact of life. Conflicts stem from many sources: people may hold different values; they may argue over property; they may miscommunicate; or accidents may lead to competing claims. My concern is with how people respond to conflict. What do people do to try to resolve disputes, and why do they choose one strategy of conflict management over another?

In a very broad sense, this parallels my earlier work in collective responses to crime in urban America (Podolefsky and DuBow 1981; Podolefsky 1983). There I assumed crime exists and examined responses to it; the questions involved the crime prevention options open to community groups and the reasons they made particular choices. I was cautious about prematurely defining "community crime prevention activities" and thereby failing to examine programs that citizens undertook in order to "do something about crime" but that I might not have viewed as an anticrime effort (like summer school for youth). In the same way, I want to be as broad as possible in the study of how Simbu respond to a grievance.

This book is about Simbu law. But why then do I discuss how Simbu respond to a grievance or ways to resolve conflict? The reason is that law, though a small word, is a big concept and may mean different things to different people. In fact, to most of us it means written rules, judges, and courtrooms. But if that is what we mean by law, and if we want to study it in New Guinea, then we have a problem.

THE PROBLEM OF "LAW"

Anthropologists, geographers, historians, and political scientists, among others, have studied many New Guinea Highland societies since their discovery. These researchers often reported high frequencies of intercommunity fighting despite close ties of kinship, marriage, and exchange between groups. They described warfare as chronic, incessant, or endemic; people simply accepted it as part of social life. In at least major portions of the Highlands, warfare was one of the most continuous and violent on record.

When people think about New Guinea warfare, they often conjure up images of head-hunting or cannibalism. An early pictorial account in the *Illustrated London News* (December 29, 1934) is titled "Never Before Seen by White Men: Cannibals' Villages in New Guinea." Years later, in the ninth volume of the Smithsonian Institution War Background Studies, Sterling (1943) writes: "Headhunters and cannibals a generation ago, most of the natives of British New Guinea have now become so accustomed to the ways of the whites that they have been trained as workers and even to assist in administering the white man's law."

I cannot deny that warfare was frequent and deadly and remains a concern today (see Podolefsky 1984). But warfare *between* groups does not mean that there is no law *within* them. Researchers have recorded many flamboyant wars, but have written very little about the less violent aspects of strained social relations.

The study of customary law is the most conspicuously neglected aspect of Highlands ethnography. There are two reasons for this: the style of colonial rule and the social structure of indigenous communities. In contrast to many colonial territories where native law and custom were officially recognized and justice was administered through formally constituted "native courts" (thus encouraging the study of traditional legal systems), the colonial administration in Papua New Guinea favored direct rule. While lower courts were directed to apply native custom, except where it was repugnant to the laws of the territory, the Native Customs (Recognition) Ordinance did not take effect until 1963. Even more striking, no native tribunals were set up to administer customary law. Thus the style of colonial administration discouraged research into customary law.

The form of traditional social organization, particularly the lack of institutions such as kingship or chieftainship and the lack of judicial mechanisms like our own or those of many parts of Africa, also discouraged the study of customary law. The colonial administrators saw nothing that looked to them like a legal system.

Concepts and definitions also affect the study of law. Can I, for example, speak of law in a society that has no written rules to judge by or judges to impose punishments? While Pospisil (1958) was able to describe Kapauku law, some scholars believed that "law" did not exist in New Guinea Highlands societies. Pospisil himself notes that had he adopted Radcliffe-Brown's definition of law (the systematic application of force . . .), he would have reported that the Kapauku had no law. Koch suggests that military operations indicate the absence, inadequacy, or breakdown of other procedures designed to settle conflicts (Koch 1970). And Hatanaka reports that "the developed concept of 'law' and related notions are not easily applicable to activities in the traditional societies of New Guinea. There is a virtual absence of authority, leadership, and law as usually understood" (Hatanaka 1973:61–62).

Certainly this is not the place to reopen the old debate over the definition of law. But I do want to point out that during the 1950s, when anthropologists first began writing about the Highlands, there were widely varying definitions of law. On the one hand law was thought to encompass a broad range of social control mechanisms, while on the other hand law was restricted to social control through the systematic application of the force of a politically organized society. Researchers that agreed with the latter definition argued that New Guinea societies lacked "law." Those that agreed with the former definition would study order and social control through a variety of mechanisms ranging from socialization to suicide.

Part of the problem in doing social science research, particularly that of the cross-cultural variety, is the problem of words and their meanings. When we use words that are part of our everyday folk vocabulary (like *law*), we find that each term brings with it its own set of connotations and meanings—its own baggage, so to speak. If we try to solve this problem by introducing new words with more precise definitions, readers accuse us of using too much jargon. Of course some disciplines introduce new words, such as *quarks, ergs,* or *neutrinos,* and it seems to be acceptable. For conversations within a culture, folk words are fine, but when we study other cultures we may need to define special terms. Do the Simbu have law? I would certainly be ill advised to call them lawless just because they do not have a legal system that looks like ours. That would be ethnocentric, and it would also bring to mind the wrong image of Simbu social life.

During the midsixties legal anthropologists turned away from ill-fated attempts to produce a single definition of law. They focused instead on the procedures people in particular societies normally use to try to settle a conflict (see Gulliver 1963; Nader 1965; Epstein 1967). The anthropological study of law is not the study of legal apparatus but the study of law *in* society.

LAW IN SOCIETY

I am not surprised that Western forms of law are not found in New Guinea. Systems which function to control people's behavior or to deal with conflicts once they erupt must fit with other aspects of the particular society. Whereas we separate our legal system from other social institutions (such as religion), people who live in small-scale, face-to-face communities integrate procedures for handling disputes into the larger social and cultural system. Just as there are no separate buildings marked "courthouse," so there are no formal institutions specifically charged with maintaining law and order. Rather, people control and respond to social transgressions through informal processes involving members of the local community. Some disputes remain disputes between individuals, whereas others, over the same kinds of issues, expand into confrontations between groups. Expansion or containment of a dispute may depend less on the grievance itself than on the relative position of the individual or groups in the social organization and on the history of relations between them.

Among the Simbu, there are no local police or other formally authorized agents of social control charged with the duty of bringing offenders before the bar of public opinion. Without such institutions, conventional wisdom might lead us to suppose that retribution or coercion is the most common way people handle trouble. However, coercion, in the form of violence, is not as frequent as one might anticipate. Anthropological theory suggests an explanation. Most disputes occur among kin and neighbors who are involved in long-term, face-to-face relationships: because geographic mobility is limited, these people must continue such relationships over long periods of time.

Suppose for a moment that you were living in New York City. Driving home from work one evening, you spot a cat dash into the road. You jam on your brakes, and before you know it the car behind you slams into your rear bumper. The cat made it across the street, and you don't seem badly injured. You get out of the car and face the other driver. Since this is New York City, it's very unlikely the person you are facing is someone you know. It is a stranger. Your first concern is getting your car fixed. Who is going to pay for it? If you have seen a lawyer's commercial lately, you might be holding your neck just to see if you can get something else out of the stranger. You don't mind a conflict if that's what it takes to get the bills covered; you don't mind putting your lawyer onto him; and you don't care if he doesn't like you. He wasn't your friend to begin with.

But what if you live in a very small town. It is probably someone you know that is behind you, quite possibly Uncle Bill. Now the situation is different. You want your car fixed, but you want to maintain relations with Uncle Bill. You remember all those Christmas gifts he brought you as a child. Certainly you aren't about to begin yelling "whiplash" without good reason.

The smaller the society the closer the relations. To understand the difference between these two situations, we need to understand the social relationships involved, not the source of the conflict. When I used the social epithets *uncle* in one case and *stranger* in the other, I played on your understanding of your own culture. The kin term *uncle* has a meaning involving expected behaviors. When you go to another culture you must discover which relations are important and what they mean in terms of proper behavior—rights and obligations.

Social relations may be defined by the position within the social structure or by actions and events. Relationships are never static, although they may seem to be. Disputes seldom occur in a social vacuum. As a dispute goes through stages of argument and agreement, social relationships are altered. Should you choose to file an obviously phoney whiplash case against Uncle Bill, you can be sure the relationship will change. Relations may be permanently changed, and such realignments may result in new relations of cooperation or conflict. The outcome and processing of a dispute, in effect, defines or redefines statuses, rights, and obligations between persons and groups (Gulliver 1969a:16).

The events described at the beginning of this chapter are a case in point. The attack of Sine and Gui on old Sago was not an isolated incident but a response to a previous affront (as we will discuss in greater detail in a later chapter). Although a meeting was held later that day, these events had long-term effects on the relations between the individuals as well as their families. The social relationship, defined by the kinship ties between the three men, was redefined by behavior inappropriate to their status as kinsmen.

Disputes in face-to-face communities arise as a complex series of events rather than as isolated acts. Each dispute is part of a long and complex history of relations between individuals and groups. Some grievances, such as insult, are easily seen as a stage in an ongoing conflict. But people can also take offense if an enemy's animals damage their crops. Even though the animal had no knowledge of past interpersonal conflicts, this can complicate and alter the social relations between disputants.

While conflicts have long and complex histories, *dispute cases* emerge as responses to some act or event—a *precipitating incident*. Whether accident or purposeful action, an event is needed to ignite the flames of conflict. There are always alternative means of handling a case once a person is embroiled in a dispute. The victim may, for example, choose coercion, mediation, or magic. The distribution of cases reveals patterns of behavior. Under what conditions do people retaliate violently; when do they use magic; and when do they negotiate? "The number of paths a dispute could conceivably follow is, of course, very large. . . . Nevertheless, in every society most of the disputes will fall into a relatively limited number of patterns" (Abel 1974:228–229).

But how do these patterns come about? They are the end result of a *series* of individual choices (see Collier 1975:128). As I analyze the distribution of cases in later chapters, I will reveal patterns that result from choices made by the people involved.

One factor that affects individual decisions is the social distance between individuals and groups. Greater social distance results in less efficient settlement mechanisms and less concern with maintaining relations. When disputants are members of different groups, there is a greater likelihood the conflict will escalate into a political contest. Indeed, disputes often serve the political interests of individuals, and disputes between individuals may expand into confrontations between groups.

Social relations also affect decisions about what kind of outcome disputants find acceptable. The contrast is sometimes drawn between all or nothing and compromise outcomes. Generally, researchers have argued that all disputes in stateless societies (Bohannan 1965:39), or at least those involving persons involved in multiplex (Gluckman 1955) or highly valued (Gulliver 1963) relationships, are settled by compromise. This is not always the case in the New Guinea Highland's. In later chapters, I will examine cases where individuals stubbornly refuse to settle a dispute, as well as cases where disputants give generous payments or gifts to bring an end to conflict. These are not random behaviors, nor are they necessarily the result of personal traits of individuals; they are part of the pattern relating conflict management to social and cultural factors.

Throughout this book I am concerned with choices about what procedure Simbu use to handle a particular dispute, what style of behavior they exhibit as the case proceeds, and what they consider a desirable, or at least acceptable, outcome. To understand disputing we need to see it as a process that happens over time. At 7:00 A.M. Sine and Gui are attacking old Sago; by 9:00 A.M. they are talking with a mediator; at 11:00 A.M. they are on their way to the police station at the government patrol post. All this time people are interacting: talking, yelling, waving arms, sitting sullenly, or parading about the ceremonial ground. These styles of behavior have meanings. People make decisions about style of behavior and acceptable outcomes throughout the process rather than at a single point in time. As a transactional process, each verbal interaction has the potential to alter the disputants' perception of the situation, suggesting that previous decisions (goals) be reevaluated. Decisions about the choice of procedure—mediation, sorcery, or violence, for example—tend to occur at particular points in the process.

My goal, in this work, is to identify and explain the criteria that people use to make choices. Obviously, I must focus on factors that come before those choices. This is, of course, a requisite of causation. When a dispute occurs, numerous social factors guide the initial decisions. I refer to the sum-total of these factors as the *grievance situation*.

The offended party enters into the grievance situation the moment he or she learns of the specific offense, whether deciding to pursue the matter publicly, privately, or not at all. Suppose, for example, a woman goes to her garden early one morning and finds that her neighbor's pig has broken into her garden and eaten some of her crops. She would, at this point, have entered into a grievance situation. This would not yet be considered a "dispute" by Gulliver (1969a:14), who reserves the term for conflict in the public arena. However, she must, at this point, decide how to proceed. Will she speak to the neighbor privately (negotiation), shoot the pig (coercion), or call for a moot (mediation)? Is she angry or understanding? What does she want out of the case?

When the behaviors of individuals during such situations are analyzed and compared, the analysis reveals those factors that are of primary importance in defining the situation and therefore influencing behavior.

I divide factors that define the grievance situation into two categories: the nature of the grievance and the social context of the dispute. Some argue that in New

Guinea disputes have such complex histories and relationships are so intricately intermeshed that it is impossible to classify cases by the type of offense. I disagree. The nature of the precipitating incident, homicide versus property damage, for example, must be considered an important variable for understanding how the offended party chooses to respond. It is theoretically possible that the nature of the offense has no effect on dispute processing, but this is unlikely. Moreover, this is an empirical question. We must ask: what is the range and variation of offenses; what are their frequencies; and how are specific offenses perceived? Do some offenses, such as adultery, tend to create greater breaches in the social fabric than do other offenses, such as damage to crops by foraging animals?

The second category of variables within the grievance situation is the social context of the dispute. An individual perceives and interprets the actions of others in terms of the social relationships and interests of the parties involved. These relationships are affected by social structure and history. What was the kinship relation between Sine, Gui, and old Sago, and how did they get along before this conflict?

Structural effects result from the relative position of disputants in the social structure (aunt/niece, for example). This position, what anthropologists call *status*, defines rights, obligations, and expected behaviors (roles). In a society composed of segmentary groups conceived in a kinship idiom, we may speak of the structural distance between groups (see chapter 2). Structural distance provides a measure of how closely related two groups are. Persons who are members of the same subclan, for example, may be said to be structurally closer than members of the same clan who are members of different subclans. Except that social structure here relates more to kinship than geography, this is like saying that people from the same neighborhood are closer than people from the same town, who are closer than folks from the same county, state, and nation.

To determine the effects of structural distance on dispute handling, I will examine the rights, obligations, and expectations underlying relations between individuals at each level of segmentation (tribe, clan, subclan). Moreover, I will contrast the importance placed on social solidarity and maintaining ongoing relations at each level. In other words, the analysis of law requires an understanding of the social structure. I will address this in the chapter that follows.

The second aspect of the social context of a dispute is the effect arising from the past history of relations between individual disputants and the groups they belong to. This includes factors like the history of past and present disputes, cooperative activities between persons and groups, friendships, and ties through marriage.

Individuals who find themselves in a grievance situation make initial choices about how best to proceed. However, the actual processing of the dispute, as when Sine and Gui attacked old Sago, may produce changes in the grievance situation. The issue under dispute itself may be redefined as may the relationship between the parties involved. Sine and Gui's attack was a reaction to what they had perceived as an offense, and it transformed the issue from trespass to personal injury. Moreover, it made old Sago wonder whether he should treat them as close kin. The transactional nature of the disputing process necessitates that individual disputants continually reevaluate the grievance situation and gauge their actions according to these reevaluations.

THE RESEARCH ADVENTURE

I have raised questions about law and conflict management that can only be studied in certain ways. I cannot experiment with human societies, nor can I mail out questionnaires or dial up survey respondents in New Guinea. To do the necessary research, to answer the questions I have raised, I had to go to New Guinea, had to live among the Simbu (previously spelled Chimbu), and had to observe their lives firsthand. This is the way of the anthropologist.

Each discipline tends toward particular research strategies. Historians work

Marriage initiates a series of gift exchanges between the families of the bride and groom. Here, while Ronnie and Noah look on, Dowa supervises the preparations of pork that will be distributed to the bride's family at a ceremony the next day.

Ronnie with some of the women of Mul

in archives. Psychological research is most often associated with experimental designs. Sociologists generally do questionnaires and telephone surveys. Anthropologists usually do ethnographic field research and participant observation.

Ethnography is both a process and a product. An anthropologist does ethnography (conducts ethnographic research) and then writes an ethnography (a book). Ethnographic research required that I go to the field, live among the people, and participate in the everyday affairs of the community. My goal was to be as unobtrusive as humanly possible. Anthropologists try to get behind the mask, to see the world as the people see it, and to understand it from their point of view.

Whenever I see a photograph of my family, my wife or my year-old, blond-haired, blue-eyed son, among a group of Simbu, I realize how difficult it is to be unobtrusive under fieldwork conditions. When I stood talking to a group of people, I saw a group of Simbu. They, however, could not help but see a group of Simbu and one pale outsider. The clothes I wore were different. The house I built was different. Yet, after a while, I believe, they looked past these superficial differences.

Anthropological fieldwork is a very personal and rewarding experience. One enters a community as a stranger and leaves some months or years later as a friend. Looking back on it, I must have been a strange and funny sight, sitting on a banana leaf, a log, or right in the mud, wearing khaki shorts and hat, scribbling in a small book and shifting layers of carbon paper every time I turned the page. I'll never know exactly why they put up with me, my wife, and son, except that maybe it brought some humor to their lives.

My wife and I spent weeks building a house and learning the basics of getting

Home Sweet Home

along with the Simbu. During that time a bond of friendship and trust grew up between ourselves and our hosts. Over time I slowly developed the rapport necessary to feel like I was at least marginally accepted. One day Kuria told me something that I thought was important for my research. I told him that I found what he said interesting and asked if he would mind if I wrote it down. Of course he didn't. The next day the same thing happened with someone else, and a day later with a third person. A few days later I was standing outside my house when a man came up to me and told me he had something interesting to report. "Take out your notebook and write this down," he said. I knew then that I was on my way to being accepted.

After the initial phase of settling in and developing rapport was over, I began the serious work of formal data collection. I collected genealogies and life histories, observed ceremonies and rituals, and interviewed a variety of people. These standard research methods flowed naturally as part of day-to-day life in the community.

In addition to these routine activities, every study makes use of particular research methods based on the questions it asks and the theoretical orientation it pursues. My study called for the use of the case method. This approach to understanding law focuses on the detailed analysis of dispute cases. As Hoebel (1942:966) pointed out, "Primitive law, like common law, must draw its generalizations from particulars which are cases, cases, and more cases." Case materials can provide concrete information on substantive rules and sanctions, and they document the legal process. The process of resolving conflict exemplifies the dynamics of a culture at work. From the particulars of a number of cases, we can arrive at general statements about law in society. Cases, as such, are not ends in themselves but the basis for analysis.

I found three analytically distinct sources of case material: government records, memory cases, and observed cases.

Magistrates at the Gumine patrol post heard cases and recorded them in official records. Although court records provided easy access to large quantities of data, I approached them with caution. I did not know how cases reached these government courts or whether they represented all types of cases that occur at the local level. For this reason, I did not assume that the case material found in the court records provided an accurate pattern of dispute behavior. I kept these data distinct from other types of cases and used them for purposes of comparison. I shall have more to say about this in chapter 4.

I use memory cases and government patrol reports to increase the time depth by providing information on past social relations. People remember selectively, and I cannot assume that memory cases, no matter how fully recorded, represent the pattern of disputes in the recent, let alone the traditional, times. Furthermore, most people recall only a personal view of conflict. Many of the intergroup animosities that remain today are the result of past grievances. Typically, people forget the details of what happened and even the nature of the original offense. Even when they claim to recall why a fight began, witnesses interviewed independently often disagree. Anthropologists (see Bernard, Killworth, Kronenfeld, and Sailer 1984) and victimologists have shown that people are not very good at accurately recalling past events. Their work is persuasive. I, therefore, exercise caution in the use of memory cases.

The most complete source of data on any particular case, and the best approximation of the actual pattern of disputes, comes from observing cases as they happen. I planned to live in the community, observe disputes, and follow each one through whatever procedures were used to handle it. Although cases were generally brought to one of the four leading men who lived near to my house, disputes sometimes occurred at one of the other hamlets or elsewhere. This presented problems that are inherent in the collection of observed dispute cases.

The settlement pattern, geography, and the transiency of the dispute phenomenon are the basic difficulties. The Simbu are widely dispersed over an extremely rugged and mountainous terrain. They do not live in villages. There was no way for me to wander randomly over the mountains hoping to hear disputes. Although, at first, I made day-long trips further into the "bush," I found that this was not an efficient way to observe dispute cases. I often learned, after returning, that I had missed a case while I was gone.

Disputes are a transient phenomenon. Two disputants bring a case to the ceremonial ground, talk it out, and then go their own ways. Unlike the collection of kinship and other sorts of anthropological data, I could not return at a later date to record what I had missed. Recording a case that occurred even a few hours earlier presents some of the problems inherent in memory cases. I could not observe the actions, attitudes, tones of voice, and the actual dialogue of the case. After long and careful consideration of the alternatives, I chose to remain in the central region around Mul, moving between those three or four areas where disputes were frequently discussed.

These considerations raise the issue of sampling and representativeness. I can be fairly certain that I heard almost all of the cases that were discussed publicly in the central portion of the tribal territory. This includes all those cases that occurred between persons who live in this area as well as those brought to this area for public debate. I do not believe that any particular type of grievance was hidden from me. I am less certain to what extent the time that I lived in Mul is typical, though I have no reason to suspect that this time was unusual except for my presence. Moreover, I am unable to ascertain, at this point, to what degree the patterns and processes revealed in the following analysis are representative of other areas of the Simbu Province.

In all, I recorded sixty-five dispute cases; most were taped and transcribed into my field notebook. Neither note-taking nor tape-recording appeared to alter people's behavior. Some cases were not fully recorded. Reasons include equipment difficulties, arriving in the middle of a dispute, or too many people talking or shouting at the same time, making transcription impossible. By recording and transcribing the disputes verbatim, I gained insights into why people chose particular courses of action that, I feel, would not otherwise have been possible.

These sixty-five cases, supplemented by information gained through participant observation, interviews, and the collection of life histories and genealogies, are the data upon which this analysis is based. Although only a small proportion of the cases are detailed in the text, I have incorporated all sixty-five cases into the tables and the flow diagram that describes the options for pursuing a grievance.

Whatever begins must somehow end, and so it is with the research adventure. At some point, it is time to pack up your patrol box and head home. Leaving the field is not fraught with the same sort of uncertainties that plague the first days, but it does raise new dilemmas. I had grown to respect, admire, and call friend many of the people of Mul. We had laughed and cried together, built houses, and broken bread. The people of Mul had shared with me their history, their beliefs, and their values. Through their lessons, I had grown as I could not have done without them. As we exchanged gifts, I wondered whether I would ever return, and if I did what it would be like. What does the outside world hold in store for the people of Mul? What wonders and what sorrows?

CONCLUSION

Anthropological research brings together three overlapping domains: a topical question, a geographic area, and a research strategy. My topic is law and conflict resolution. I ask a simple question: how do individuals resolve conflicts in the absence of formal legal systems and authorities? Unresolved, conflicts destroy society; conflicts within the family destroy the family; conflicts within the community destroy the community; and conflicts within the nation destroy the nation. Conflict resolution mechanisms, therefore, function to protect the social system. They repair rips in the social fabric by preserving social relationships between people and groups.

There are other perspectives. Some theoretical orientations would draw attention to the way that formal legal systems also maintain systems of power and inequality. Other orientations show how conflict between groups enhances the solidarity within each of them.

My interests led me to select a particular area of the world as the geographic focus of my study. Papua New Guinea societies lack authoritarian offices and formal legal institutions. The topic and geographic area limited my choice of research methods. I am glad they did; there is nothing quite like the experience of anthropological fieldwork.

Because we are looking at the role of law in society, I begin by examining Simbu culture and social relations. Who are the Simbu; where and how do they live; what are their beliefs, values and ideologies; and how do these affect their actions and behaviors?

2 / Simbu Culture and Society

The people of Mul today live poised on a precipice, about to tumble into a global world that they know almost nothing about. Within a lifetime, only a few decades, in fact, they have emerged from Stone Age conditions. Metal working, basket making, and pottery were unknown. Men felled trees with stone axes and women planted gardens using digging sticks. There was no census and no taxation, no presidents or premiers, chiefs or landlords. Today a few young men own radios. Several of the local children walk three miles or more each way for a bit of education provided at the school on the government station. Men own small numbers of coffee trees and from them earn cash that all too often is spent on beer imported during harvest season. Increasingly clothed in the torn and unwashed trappings of Western civilization, the people of Mul follow a steady path from "tribesmen" to peasants.

But the surface changes more readily than the core. Superficial transformations visible to the naked eye mask the underlying stability of ecology, economy, social organization and structure, values and ideology. Certainly changes have been brought by the introduction of new social institutions, but these institutions and their effects must be understood within the context of the traditional society. Law is a particular example.

Western law has come, in an official sense, as far as the government station at Gumine three miles west of Mul. Here there is a large grass-roofed building used as a courthouse. During the first part of my stay, court was heard by the Australian district officer in charge. During the second half, a Papua New Guinean magistrate was assigned to the Gumine District Court. The existence of police and a western style court had its effects on how dispute cases were handled in Mul, as we shall see, but very few of the disputes that erupted in Mul were taken out of the community to the formal agents of social control at the government station. Just as dispute cases remained physically within the local community, so must our understanding of the legal process be grounded in fundamental knowledge of the traditional society and culture. This chapter provides the necessary background on the Simbu people.

BACKGROUND

The Simbu Province is an area of 2,270 square miles (5,879 square kilometers) containing an indigenous population of about 160,000. I lived and worked in the central portion of the province (see map 2). The area can be found at 6 degrees 12 minutes south latitude, 144 degrees 57 minutes east longitude.

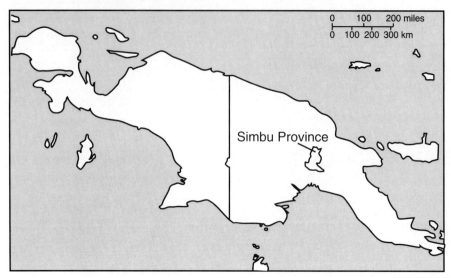

Location of the Simbu Province

Mul, the community that is the geographic focus of this study, lies approximately three miles east of the Gumine District Headquarters. The provincial capital, Kundiawa, is thirty-two miles north of Gumine. While Kundiawa is only thirty-two miles from Gumine, it was several hours' drive in good weather. If the rain was too heavy, as it often was, even the four-wheel-drive Land Cruisers had to turn around, postponing the trip for another day. Kundiawa itself reminded me of a frontier town. There were several paved streets, a number of trade stores, a tourist hotel, a tiny air strip, and a Christian book store, the owners of which gave us a place to stay when we first arrived.

The Gumine District Headquarters consisted of a post office, a medical aid post, a courthouse, a trade store, and several police barracks. We lived in one of these barracks for several weeks while we looked for a place to make a more permanent home. I was introduced to a young man who could speak a bit of English, a very little bit of English, and I could speak a bit of pidgin, a very little bit of pidgin. Each day he and I would set out from Gumine in a different direction, looking for that ideal spot. As we walked those trails we would pass women and young children herding pigs and men shouldering machetes, axes, and, occasionally, bows and arrows or spears. When our son was with us, the older women often smiled and, clenching their fist to their breast, said, "Ayee." I didn't know what that meant, but I assumed it was a greeting. It struck me years later that I never did ask what that particular sound and gesture meant. It seems to be true that a smile is a smile the world over. At the same time it took me a good while to get used to people around me carrying deadly weapons. Tromping through the mud, I found those early days an emotional roller coaster: filled with exhilaration at the mere fact of being in the field and confusion about how to handle the day-to-day things that were so different from home.

Woman and child

We might have gone farther from Kundiawa, but I wanted to work among the Simbu people, and as you go farther south you come to the Karamui District. The people of the Karamui, the southernmost district in the province, are socially and culturally different. Though the people of the Gumine District are located halfway between the Central Simbu and the Karamui, their culture and social arrangements approximate, in most respects, those of the central Simbu.[1]

Mul is the name given to a vaguely defined core area within a larger tribal territory. When in Kundiawa, Mul residents may identify themselves as being from Gumine. If they wish to be more specific, the term *Mul* may be used to indicate the region east of the Gumine government station. Within the local area, however, Mul has more precise meaning, though it does not denote either a territorial of kin group.

The history of contact between outsiders and the people of Gumine is quite recent. Foot patrols into the Gumine region began in the late 1940s and continued through the early 1950s. The colonial government established a patrol post at Gumine during the middle of the 1950s, which was elevated to subdistrict

The road from Kundiawa to Mul

headquarters in 1966. Mul is the site of the first rest house east of the Gumine government station. In earlier times government patrols headed for other regions made brief stopovers at Mul. The rest house has now fallen down, but the site remains a focal point for government activities such as tax collecting and voting. During the early 1950s, Lutheran and Catholic missions were established several hours' walk from Mul. During the early 1960s, a dirt road was constructed from Kundiawa to Gumine, and shortly afterward it was extended through Mul. And what an amazing road it is, climbing steeply over the tortuous terrain, one hairpin turn after another. Indeed, the experience of our four-wheel-drive Land Cruiser, axle-deep in mud, sliding backward down the mountain, only to try again and again, will long remain a vivid memory of my first hair-raising trip from Kundiawa to Gumine.

It once again strikes me how recently this all occurred. Regular and fairly frequent contact with the outside world began only ten to fifteen years before my family and I arrived. Can we even begin to imagine the pace of transformation and how it affected people? Although simple to us Americans, building a road into a community can set in motion transformations that will have profound consequences.

With the road came many changes. Although the dirt road is still often impassable, it allowed people to plant cash crops and transport them to market. Some men have spent periods in coastal towns working as wage laborers. An elementary school was established at the Gumine government station in 1963. Even today, however, students who continue their education beyond the elementary level must live in either Kerowagi or Chuave, a long distance to the north. A small number of young men have taken courses at the university; out of a tribe of nearly four thousand, one person had completed technical college at Rabaul.

Thirteen languages are spoken in the Simbu Province, with language groups

Changing fashions of "dressing up"

ranging in size from 66,000 to 1,500 speakers. The people who live in Mul speak Golin, the second-largest language group (26,700 speakers). This linguistic diversity makes it difficult to speak to other Simbu who live more than a few miles away. Pidgin English has recently been introduced as a *lingua franca* that allows people from throughout Papua New Guinea to communicate with one another. In Mul most men between the ages of ten and forty are able to hold a conversation in pidgin; in the forty to fifty-year age bracket, most men have some understanding of pidgin and are able to utter a few words, whereas old men neither understand nor speak pidgin. Though some of the young and middle-age women seem to understand pidgin, few admit to it, and very few speak the language.

I am trying to project a picture of a community in transition. While Mul hurtles headlong into the modern, post-colonial era, culture and social life remain strongly traditional. During my first trips to Gumine I learned of tribal warfare only a few miles to the west of the government station. I was tempted to initiate my study of conflict in that area, but I was concerned that the study would inevitably be drawn into a focus on warfare rather than law, and also that I might be suspected of government or police affiliations and therefore be unable to develop the level of rapport I felt necessary to the research. My explorations to the east of the government station eventually brought me to Mul, one of the most densely populated areas in all of New Guinea.

ENVIRONMENT AND POPULATION

Since the late nineteenth century, scholars have thought that population density affects the evolution of legal complexity. More dense populations exert greater

Warfare brings death, and death brings sorrow. Here Ronnie treats a man who cut off part of his finger as an act of mourning for a slain relative.

pressure on land. Under the weight of population pressure, people employ complex agricultural techniques and more intensive labor to grow sufficient food to support themselves. Land becomes scarce and highly valued. With increasing population density and agricultural intensity emerge individual, private ownership of land (Brown and Podolefsky 1976). This places an additional burden on law to protect individual rights of private property. Or at least so the theory goes (see Podolefsky 1987).

With an average population density of 271 persons per square mile, Mul is among the most densely populated areas in all of New Guinea. The density on cultivatable land is about 295 people per square mile. This is drastically different from regions such as the Karamui, where the density is less than 20 per square mile, or the lower-altitude fringe highlands, where densities may average less than half a person per mile.

You might think that the people of Mul would migrate and resettle in lower-density areas where land and resources are more plentiful, but this has not occured. Disease was an important factor influencing the traditional population distribution. The low-altitude districts south of Mul apparently had far higher mortality rates, most likely due to malaria, among other ills. The Simbu attributed the frequent deaths to witchcraft, sorcery, or spirits, and these areas gained a reputation as bad places to live. This is the major reason people with land rights in the south give for not resettling there permanently. Other explanations include the lack of schools, medical aid posts, and access to roads for bringing cash crops to market.

The mountainous terrain further compounds the problem of crowding. Geographically, Mul lies just south of the gorge of the Marigl River at an elevation of about 5,500 feet. The land rises steeply to a ridge running east-west at an elevation of about 8–9,000 feet. Even though Mul lies just south of the equator, the altitude keeps the climate quite pleasant; the daily average of about seventy degrees remains fairly constant year-round though the temperature drops to about fifty degrees each night. The cold nighttime temperatures require the Simbu to make fires in their houses, which consumes what has become one of Simbu's scarcest resources—wood.

Unlike America, where seasons change from hot to cold, the seasons in New Guinea vary from wet to dry (actually wet and not so wet would be better descriptions). During the wet season, it rains every day, and even in the dry season it rains every few days. This climate allows the staple food crops to be grown year-round without particular planting and harvest seasons. There never was, therefore, any need for the Simbu to develop means to store harvested crops for extended periods.

The Simbu grow their crops on slopes rising from the river gorge to the mountain ridge, using a method known as slash-and-burn agriculture. Ideally, men cut down and burn forest trees, which returns nutrients to the soil. Gardens are planted and after two or three harvests the garden is abandoned and a new forest plot is cleared and planted. Over time, grass, then scrub brush, then trees regrow and the forest returns to its original condition. After thirty-five years or so the trees are mature and are ready to be cut down so new gardens can be planted. This system allows continuous agriculture without degrading the soil and without the use of fertilizers.

Unfortunately, this ideal is no longer a possibility in Mul. With the high population density, people do not have the luxury of enough land to allow garden plots to remain fallow for thirty-five years. There is simply not enough land to rotate through this cycle without coming back to a garden plot before it has had sufficient time to rejuvenate. Most garden land is left fallow for only about seven years before the owners are pressed into replanting. Without the time to fully recuperate, the quality of the soil declines. People complain that the soil is turning red and is not as fertile as it once was.

The problem of overpopulation is exacerbated by raising pigs and cash crops. While pigs are slaughtered for a variety of reasons, the fact remains that pigs, like people, consume garden-grown produce and therefore put more pressure on land. Pigs are allowed to roam free to forage for food, and one of their favorite foods is the sweet potatoes being grown in Simbu gardens. As we shall see, these garden-

Overpopulation has led to scarcity of trees. Here, because he has no trees for making fences, old Sago digs a trench to keep free-roaming pigs out of his garden.

gate crashers are the most frequent source of conflict among neighbors. A yearly increase in the number of coffee trees, which are grown as a cash crop, places additional pressure on land because less land is available for gardens.

Most of us do not imagine that technologically simple societies struggle with some of the same problems that are seen as global issues for the industrial world. Yet here, in the lush mountains of New Guinea, we find people who, like ourselves, are witnessing firsthand the problem of overpopulation. They recognize the strain it places on their local environment, frequently saying that there are just too many people. Like ourselves, they are pushing the environmental limits of a sustainable future.

One of the things society does, through social and cultural rules about such things as inheritance, for example, is to organize the distribution of people on the land. How do people and groups attain and maintain ownership of property, and who has access to it? How do people become and remain members of groups that control territory? This is part of what is called social organization. We will find that Simbu society is organized quite differently than our own. Understanding the relationships and expected behaviors of people, as defined by membership in a social group, is an important foundation for understanding law in society.

SOCIAL ORGANIZATION

If you ask someone from Mul about the origins of their tribe, they will tell you some version of the following story. Once upon a time there was a man named Nemeri Temi who lived, with his wife, about ten miles west of Mul in an area called Yani. Nemeri and his wife had several sons, who set out to begin new groups. Among these children was a man named Kobulaku, who married and had four sons: Naraku, Malaku, Egaku, and Kunaraku. Each of these had sons of their own. Here the consistency of the story breaks down. Some people know all the names of Malaku's sons, but few of the sons of the others. Other people know the names of Naraku's sons, but not the other sons, and so on.

This story uses kinship to describe the origin of social groups in Mul. It provides a framework to explain the social and political organization. We do not use kinship to describe our social and political organization, but suppose we did. We might have a story that went something like this. Once upon a time there was a man named George Washington (after whom the capital was named). George had fifty children: Virginia, Maryland, Arizona, Kentucky, and so on. Each of these people had many children, whose names bear a striking resemblance to the names of the counties, and each of these had children whose names correspond to the names of the cities and towns in each county. We quickly recognize the descendants of George Washington as the names of the territorial political units of state, county, and city or town. Like the families descended from Nemeri Temi, the towns are within the counties, which are within the states, which are within the nation, which is the largest political unit. An important difference is that in Simbu the people are in fact kin to other members of their group, whereas for us this would be a myth. Nevertheless, keeping this analogy in mind will help you understand Simbu social relations. If we believed in the George Washington origin story, we might very well believe that people who live in the same town should act like brothers and sisters. People from different towns within the county should act like cousins. The farther away, the more distant the relation and the less important the social relationship.

Just as we have nations, states, counties, and cities, so do the Simbu have tribes, clans, subclans, and subclan sections. Kobulaku, the name of the first ancestor who came to Mul, is also the name of the tribe, the largest political and kinship group in Mul. The tribe consists of four original clans: Naraku, Malaku, Egaku, and Kunaraku. In other words, the tribe is segmented into four clans, each clan is segmented into subclans, and each subclan is segmented into sections. When they talk about how their society is organized, the Simbu link hierarchical segments as father/son and parallel segments as brothers. Figure 2-1 gives the names of all the groups in the Kobulaku tribe and shows how they are linked.

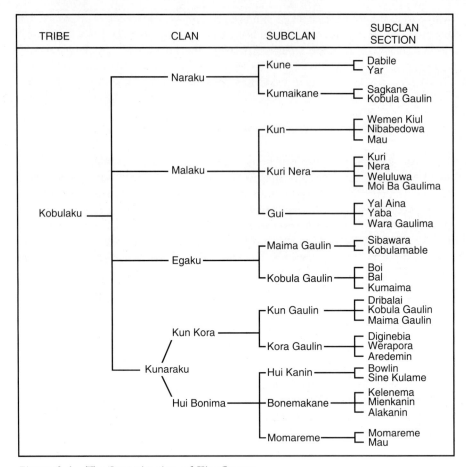

Figure 2-1   The Organization of Kin Groups

This model of Kobulaku organization appears simple and straightforward. Trying to get this sorted out in the field, however, was a source of considerable confusion and frustration. I kept getting different information from different people. Were they intentionally trying to confuse me just for the fun of it, or was I just too thick to figure out what was going on?

While everyone agreed on the name of the first founder (Nemeri Temi) and his son Kobulaku, people disagreed about the names of Kobulaku's brothers. Everybody agreed on the names of Kobulaku's sons—the names of the four clans—but the real problem came when I tried to learn the names of the groups that made up each clan. Every time I thought I had it completely right, someone politely explained, as you would to a child, that I had confused some minor point of fact.

Eventually I realized that people could accurately report the names of the subclans (and subclan sections) for their own clan but were unclear about the composition of the other clans. For example, a member of the Naraku clan would be able to report the names of the subclans as Kune and Kumaikane, but he or she would most likely admit to not knowing the Egaku subclan names or might report them incorrectly (that is, differently than they would be reported by an Egaku man or woman). Similarly, a person from Egaku would know the names of the subclans of Egaku but probably not those of Malaku or Kunaraku. Furthermore, although individuals within a particular clan were able to enumerate the subclans of their own clan and the subclan sections of their own subclan, they had difficulty identifying the names of the subclan sections of other subclans within the their own clan.

Were they trying to fool me? I think not. What became clear was that I had incorrectly assumed that I could simply ask about their social organization and they could as simply answer me as though it had been recorded in a book. I came to understand what I have since found to be true in most instances. People, whether in New Guinea or in America, seldom understand or can explain the organization or culture of their own society. That is why it takes social scientists to do it. I was expecting people to know things that they may not have any need to know. Could I have done better about my own society? While I might know all the towns in my county, I do not know the names of all the counties in the next state. In fact how many of us can name the counties in our own state? If I were pressed into answering, I might provide a list of counties, but my answers would probably be wrong, or at least incomplete. And these are mere facts. Suppose I were asked to describe the economic and power relations between city, county and, state governments—not a very realistic expectation. Social science is detective work, and, like detectives, social scientists must put together the whole story from shreds of sometimes inconsistent evidence.

I discovered that the people of Mul conceptualize their social organization as though it were a family. I could eventually draw the whole family tree, but each of them only knew the details of their own branch. The total system is seldom known to individuals, nor does this seem to be of concern to them. This is important for the study of conflict.

In the study of law and conflict, we need to know how people define appropriate behavior and how it varies for different situations and for individuals in different status relationships, such as friends, kin, and strangers. A *status* is a position in a two-person relationship (such as father/son) that identifies a set of rights and obligations. A *role* is the set of behaviors associated with a status. Suppose, for example, that a man from the Dabile section, Kune subclan of the Naraku clan (see figure 2-1), meets a man from the Mau section, Kun subclan of the Malaku clan. Their interaction (as in a dispute case) will be guided by the fact that they are from two different clans within the same tribe. There are certain rights and obligations that guide and affect the interactions between co-members of a tribe. If our first fellow meets a man from the Yar section of the Kune subclan of the Naraku clan, they will behave as members of two different sections but of the same subclan.

The men who are of the same clan but different subclans are more distantly related than the men who are of the same subclan, and rights and obligations as well as appropriate behaviors are defined by this structural distance. The closeness of a kinship relation may affect how people interact in conflict situations. Historical circumstances, such as past grievances, may affect how people interact, but this is a different variable that should, I feel, be kept distinct.

Normally, in studies of law and society, we are concerned with the actual genealogical connection between people rather than structural distance. In 1971, for example, Philip Gulliver examined the kinship chart of the Ligomba community and showed that these kinship connections explained how disputes were handled. If two people got into a dispute, someone who was structurally intermediate, that is, was between them on the kinship chart, would step in to act as a mediator. But African societies, such as that studied by Gulliver, place great importance on kinship connection.

Are genealogical relationships important for the study of conflict management in the New Guinea Highlands? We can begin to answer this question by asking whether people can identify a wide range of relatives. Table 2-1 presents the genealogical knowledge, in the male line, of a sample of eighteen men from the Mul community. I am concerned with males because the Simbu live in patrilineal patrilocal descent groups, which means that as children grow up and get married, male children will stay in the community and their wives will move in from elsewhere, whereas young women who marry will move to the community of their husbands. All the men in a community are related in the male line. Married women are connected to the men and to other women through marriage.

In this table a "+" in a column means that individuals recalled the name of their kinsman in that category. A "/" means they recalled some of the names but not all. A "0" means they had no kin in that category.

Most men knew the names of their father (F), father's brother (FB), father's

TABLE 2-1   GENEALOGICAL KNOWLEDGE IN THE MALE LINE

No.	Age	F	FB	FBC	FF	FFB	FFBC	FFF	FFFB	FFFBC
1	YM	+	+	+	+	+	+	+	+	+
2	M	+	+	+	+	/	+			
3	A	+	+	+	+			+		
4	Y	+	+	+	+	+				
5	M	+	+	+	+	+				
6	LM	+	+	+	+	+				
7	Y	+	+	+	+					
8	M	+	+	+	+					
9	LM	+	+	+	+					
10	M	+	+	+	+					
11	Y	+	+	+	+					
12	Y	+	+	+	+					
13	YM	+	+	+	+					
14	M	+	+	+	+					
15	A	+	0	0	+					
16	A	+	+	0	+					
17	A	+	+							
18	YM	+								

Age: Y—young; M—middle age; LM—late middle; A—aged

brother's children (FBC), and father's father (FF). Only five of the eighteen (28%) knew the names of their father's father's brother (FFB). And only two of the eighteen (11%) knew the names of their father's father's brother's children (FFBC; none knew the names of the FFBCC). There is no apparent correlation with age and so we can assume that the situation was not much different in the past. Simbu typically explain that if they didn't know someone, if they did not "see their face," they would not recall their name.

The important point for the study of law is that each man lives with others to whom he *believes* he is related. They call each other brothers and believe that they have "one blood." Yet, since FFB, FFBC, and FFBCC are a man's elders and peers within the group, individuals cannot trace any genealogical connection to most members within even the smallest group. I assume that since individuals are not aware of the genealogical connections, then these biological links cannot affect the individuals' behavior. And, I also assume that if individuals believe themselves to be related (as might a person whose FF was adopted into the group), this will affect their behavior even though there is no "real" genealogical connection. As sociologist W. I. Thomas (1928:572) once said, "If men [or women] define situations to be real, they are real in their consequences." Some might not make this assumption.

The implication of these findings is that it is not important, as it might be in Africa, to understand the particular genealogical connections between disputants, nor is it important to understand the total hierarchical descent construct. Rather, individuals interact in terms of oppositions and alignments between groups. We need to know the rights and obligations, expected modes of behavior, and restrictions on conflict associated with co-membership in each level of social grouping. Every conflict is between persons who are either (a) structurally unrelated (members of different tribes) or (b) co-members of a group at some level of segmentation. The second thing we need to know is the particular historical circumstances that surround the ongoing relations between groups, as these may confound the effects of structure and ideology.

Groups

Phratry and Tribe

Brown (1972) refers to the most inclusive of the Simbu segmentary groups as a *phratry*—a descent group composed of a number of supposedly related clans. Although there was little disagreement concerning the name of the phratry founder (Nemeri Temi), people did not agree on the names of the groups that compose the phratry, which is not named, and it performs no unifying functions. The general belief is one of common patrilineal descent with a vaguely defined set of groups to the west.

The Kobulaku tribe is a territorial group that encompasses almost all lands used for residence or gardening by its members. The single exception is 372 men, women, and children who live a day's walk south of the tribal territory. These people are parts of a clan that migrated south in the aftermath of intratribal warfare in precontact times. Most members of this clan have returned to the tribal territory since pacification (see below). The 3,944 members of the Kobulaku tribe, including those living to the south, combine to give food and pigs at pig feasts and, in the past, combined occasionally in warfare.

The story of how the Kobulakus came to reside at Mul has many variations. Most agree that the people who now make up the Kobulaku tribe came from the Yani area. Older men report that during the time of their great grandfathers (though one man insists that he was eight to ten years old) a fight occurred between several Yani groups over the theft of some ripe bananas. The Kobulakus were vanquished and moved east, eventually settling at Mul. Some versions of this history suggest that Kobulaku was a named group before this migration, while others argue that the clan groups were united and given a common name after they had already settled in Mul.

To the west and east of the Kobulaku tribal territory live other groups. On the north lies the Marigl River; some gardens are maintained, though with great difficulty, on the other side of the river. There is a forty-acre plot of land named Minibe that has been the subject of dispute for over twenty years and has not been cultivated during that time. To the south, the tribal territory extends into the sparsely populated "bush," and some members of the Naraku clan maintain permanent residence in Kalwari, a full day's walk south. This latter group participates fully in clan and tribal activities and a great deal of visiting occurs between the residents of Mul and Kalwari. Many of the men from Mul own pandanus nut orchards in Kalwari and, frequently, pigs owned by Mul residents are cared for by kin in Kalwari.

Clans

Clans in Simbu are territorial, named groups that are exogamous, meaning that they do not permit marriage among members of the same clan. All marriages, therefore, are between men and women who were born into different clans. Until recently the Kobulaku tribe was segmented into four clans: Naraku, Malaku, Egaku, and Kunaraku. The latter group, however, has recently split into two intermarrying clans and, hence, the name Kunaraku now refers to a linked pair of clans, Kun Kora and Hui Bonima (see figure 2-1).

The tribal territory is divided into three areas by boundaries running approximately perpendicular to the Marigl River and extending up the slopes to the ridge and into the bush. Each contains a variety of altitudinal and ecological zones. The western territory is occupied by the Kunarakus, the central portion by the Narakus and Malakus, and the eastern territory by the Egakus. Though these territorial arrangements are recognized and boundary lines can be pointed out, the areas, in reality, are defined by the distribution of individually owned plots rather than a group territory.

The Kunarakus were, until recently, a single exogamous clan. Presently, the five subclans are combined into two exogamous intermarrying groups. The subclans of Kun Gaulin and Kora Gaulin refer to themselves as Kun Kora; the subclans of Hui Kanin, Bonimakane, and Momarame refer to themselves as Hui Bonima. The former has a population of 789 and the latter 367 members. Nevertheless, members of Kunaraku refer to themselves as a single group and hold bush land in common.

When I asked why the clan had divided, I was told that when the white men came they told the Kunarakus that since they were such a large clan (present population 1,156) their members could intermarry. I inquired repeatedly as to whether there had been strife between the two segments of the original clan and each time was told that there had not. (This public denial, of course, proves nothing and may merely be a statement of present political relations.) Members of the even larger Malaku clan (present population 1,254) report that they had been given the same advice but have not, as yet, split into two intermarrying groups.

Brookfield and Brown (1963:11) have pointed out that clan fission traditionally occurs in two ways: "Defeat sometimes forced a part of a clan to migrate and sever its ties with the part that remained; . . . (or) two clan sections grew large enough to allow intermarriage, and the sections subsequently took on other functions of independent clans." The fission of Kunaraku, however, appears to be the result of outside influence. One of the resulting clans, Hui Bonima, has only 367 members and is far smaller than any of the other Kobulaku clans. Also, either because the stimulus for the split was external to the group, or because it occurred so recently, the new clans have not yet, with the exception of clan exogamy, taken on the functions of independent clans. These factors have presented some difficulty of classification; shall I follow the descent principle and refer to Kunaraku as a clan with two intermarrying sections or shall I employ the exogamic rule as the defining feature of the clan and refer to Kun Kora and Hui Bonima as linked clans? Brown's (1969:81) statement that "the clan is defined most clearly as the exogamic group" would appear to support the latter alternative for purposes of ethnographic description. During disputes, however, which are the activities I am most concerned with, members of Kunaraku speak of themselves as a single clan. Thus, when referring to "the clan" in the context of dispute behavior, the Kunaraku will be considered to be a single clan.

If Kunaraku is considered a single clan, then the Kobulaku tribe has four clans, ranging in size from 729 to 1,254, with a mean size of 986. If, on the other hand, the Kunarakus are considered to be two clans, then the tribe has five clans, ranging in size from 367 to 1,254, with a mean size of 789. All such population data were derived from census materials available at the Gumine Local Government Council office. Group populations, therefore, include all those who list themselves as members of a particular group for census purposes. This usually includes male group members, unmarried sisters, wives, and their children.

The central portion of the tribal territory is of primary importance since Mul itself lies within this area and a large portion of the disputes that form the data base in the chapters that follow involve the clans that reside and garden in this central area. The 1,254 members of the Malaku clan live intermixed with between 306 and 430 (see below) of the 802 members of the Naraku clan. The remaining Narakus live to the south in Kalwari. This settlement pattern is the result of past warfare within the tribe.

Approximately forty years ago the central area was divided into Naraku and Malaku territories. As one story has it, a group from the Yani area gave a large gift of pigs to the Kobulakus. Most of the pigs were given to the Narakus, making the Malaku and the Egaku jealous and sparking an attack against the Naraku. A second account suggests that the fight started over a stone axe. A third version reports that a Malaku woman was killed in the bush and, though the Narakus denied the charge, a fight broke out. Yet another story involves a fight between some young boys over the debt of a small pig. All the stories agree that the Malakus, aided by the Egakus, defeated the Narakus who hid among the Kunarakus, but were eventually routed by the two opposing clans.

These stories were all reported by people who were young men at the time and who claim to have actually fought in the battles. They vividly demonstrate the problem inherent in collecting memory cases of past disputes. It is difficult to determine with any degree of certainty which of the stories is correct or if the various stories together somehow form a complete picture.

In any case, all the stories agree that the combined forces of Egaku and Malaku were able to chase the Narakus south to what is referred to as the "Bomai side" of the Marigl Divide. The Narakus took up residence at Kalwari, where a portion still remain. The presence of government influence during the 1950s allowed the

Kawali demonstrates the use of the bow.

Narakus, either under the expressed or implied protection of the government, to return to Mul, where they were given land by the Malakus. This history has resulted in the present pattern of land holdings in the central area of the tribal territory and the residential division of the Naraku clan into two areas.

Not only is the Naraku clan residentially divided, but so are its subclans and their respective subclan sections. Table 2-2 shows the residential distribution of the Naraku clan. The data for table 2-2 were derived by listing all 802 members of the Naraku clan as given in the government census books, then inquiring among a group of knowledgeable informants as to the primary residence of each clan member.

The history of conflict between the Naraku and Egaku clans led me to inquire about animosities between the Narakus and other groups. Uniformly, people pointed out that these were "things from the past" and that they no longer felt any hostility toward the opposing groups. Nevertheless, during a dispute over the theft of a few rolls by an Egaku man from a trade store owned by a man of the Naraku clan, the argument became heated and these past incidents were vengefully recounted. Nothing of a similar nature occurred during disputes between the Narakus and the Malakus. This may have been fortuitous or it may be that the Narakus feel well disposed toward the Malakus since the Malakus returned, in gift form, the large plots of land on which the Naraku now reside. Moreover, since Naraku and Malaku land is intermingled within the central area, there is constant contact between members of the two clans, which allows for extensive intermarriage and mutual aid. As a result of these developments, a higher value is placed on social relations between Malaku and Naraku than between Naraku and Egaku, despite the fact that the root of the original trouble was between the Narakus and Malakus.

Clan members see themselves as a solidary group vis à vis members of other clans. In the past, clans frequently united in warfare and their members joined together in making compensatory payments to other clans for deaths occurring during warfare. Clans are responsible for paying compensation for all persons killed by their group, as well as compensating allied clans that provided aid in warfare. This same principle holds at all levels of segmentation. The failure to compensate adversary or allied groups may develop into hostility that outlasts the memory of the breach that precipitated the original conflict.

TABLE 2-2   POPULATION OF NARAKU SUBGROUPS BY TERRITORY OF RESIDENCE

| Clan | | | Naraku | | |
| Subclan | | Kune | | Kumai Kane | |
Section	Dabile	Yar	Sagkane	Kobula Gaulin	Total
Residence					
Mul	99	91	105	11	306
Kalwari	0	134	85	153	372
Both	0	0	0	124	124
Total	99	225	190	288	802

Brookfield and Brown (1963:11) point out that "intratribal competition takes the form of interclan food exchanges and display at ceremonies" and that "when a tribe visits a ceremonial ground to sing during the pig festival, it usually divides into clan units."

Subclans

Like the tribe and the clan, each subclan (ranging in size from 200 to 500 persons) is named after its founder, who is believed to have been descended in a direct line from the original phratry founder. Members of the subclan maintain a belief in common patrilineal descent. At times, especially during disputes, individuals may refer to one another as being "one-blood," though they may not, in fact, be members of the same "one-blood" group (subclan section; see below). In such instances, the "one-blood" idiom is used to symbolize the importance of a social relationship that is being threatened by the rising hostility between the disputants.

Individual plots of land owned by members of the subclan are not randomly distributed throughout the clan territory in a pattern that would result from chance alone. Rather, land owned by members of the subclan tends to be clustered in a particular portion of the clan territory. Residents are able to locate subclans by pointing toward particular ridges and their accompanying slopes. There are numerous exceptions to the trend for members of a subclan to live and garden within a single area. Though I have no quantitative data on the geographic distribution of land ownership, most people who own land outside this vaguely defined subclan area usually do so within the clan territory. As a result, the subclan is more geographically dispersed within the clan territory than the clan is within the tribal territory. Succinctly stated: "Within the tribe the fragmentation of group holding increases with segmentation" (Brookfield and Brown 1963:13).

The high population density places strains on a variety of resources. Over time, deforestation and a reduction of soil fertility has become a serious problem. Because of the lack of wood for fence building, men frequently enclose a number of individual garden plots within a single enclosure. Such cooperation is most frequent between members of the same subclan or subclan section. Plots owned by men from other subclans within the clan or other clans within the tribe are sometimes included, though not often.

The purpose of these fences is to prevent domesticated pigs that are allowed to roam freely in search of food from damaging gardens. Although it is the garden owners' responsibility to build and maintain these fences, dispute cases reveal that the owner of a pig that damages a garden is held responsible for the damages regardless of whether the fence was in good repair or not.

The subclan is active in marriage arrangements and ceremony. When a young man wishes to marry, he informs his father, his brothers, and the most influential men of his subclan section, who solicit contributions to a bride price. The goal is to collect a wealth of goods and give them to the parents of the bride. Though the majority of the large contributions come from members of the subclan section, most members of the subclan contribute. Other close relatives of the groom, such as his sisters and their husbands, are also expected to make contributions. After accepting the bride price, the parents of the bride distribute it among the members of their own subclan and subclan section. Sometime later, the bride's family will make a similar collection and give a return gift to the groom's family.

In this way, marriages initiate and maintain long-standing relationships of exchange and friendship between the individuals and their groups. Moreover, the collection and distribution of goods within the respective groups remind the members of their mutual interdependence. This serves to reinforce social solidarity within the subclan and subclan section.

Subclan Section

Each subclan is segmented into several (between two and five) subclan sections, sometimes referred to as one-blood groups. I have reasonably accurate population data for only the four sections of the Naraku clan, which range in size from 99 to 288 persons, with a mean size of 200.

The subclan section is the first unit to mobilize for warfare. These conflicts may remain between sections, or they may expand to include allied groups on either side. The *potentiality* of expansion depends on the position of the groups in the segmentary system. For example, if two sections within the same subclan came into conflict, it is unlikely that it would expand because potential allies are equally tied to both groups. On the other hand, if two sections of different clans came into conflict, it is possible that the conflict between the sections would expand into war between the clans. There is no automatic submission to this segmentary principle, however. The past relations between the groups is important. The actual recruitment of allies appears to depend heavily on interpersonal ties between individuals. I have already described, for example, the alignment of the Malaku and Egaku clans against the Narakus. In a more recent example, the death of a high school student of the Kun subclan of the Malaku clan in August 1976, led, after a delay in making the agreed-upon compensation payment, to fighting between the boy's father's subclan and his mother's subclan. Although these subclans are segments of different tribes, extensive cross-cutting ties prevented the conflict from expanding to include other groups.

The subclan section is the only group that restricts internal fighting. If co-members become extremely angry, individuals attack each other with fists, clubs, or staffs, but not with axes, arrows, or spears. We have already seen an example of this in the attack of old Sago by Sine and Gui described on the first pages of the previous chapter. As you may recall, the men had axes tucked in their belts, but, despite raging tempers, fought only with staffs. These restrictions are related to the belief that members of the subclan section are closely related genealogically and have "one-blood." Unlike most Highland societies (see Brown 1967:50–51) lethal combat occurs between sections of the subclan.

The subclan section is an important cooperative unit. Brookfield and Brown (1963:13) point out that in the Central Simbu, subclan sections may have five or

At ceremonies, such as weddings, food is given by one group to another. Before it is distributed, groups enhance their prestige by displaying the quantity of their distribution and making speeches that highlight their generosity.

more parcels of land and individuals may own one or more plots in each one of them. This pattern is also reported by members of the Mul community. Garden land enclosed within a single fence consists predominantly of plots owned by members of a particular subclan section. These men cooperate in the initial burning of the fallow cover and in the maintenance of the enclosure.

Men also cooperate in the construction of men's houses that are often, though not always, associated with a particular subclan section. Residence in the men's house is not restricted to members of the subclan section; overnight visits are frequent. During the evenings men sit in the men's house telling stories of past events and recounting the day's activities. Plans are discussed for initiating new gardens or ceremonies. There is no formality to these discussions. While some men talk, others may sleep, play cards or dice, or go off to visit. Frequently, the men can be heard singing long into the night.

Council Sago draws on his ability as an orator to focus attention on the impressive gifts of pork (16 pigs) and beef (1 cow) his group is about to distribute. In an area where people earn about one kina per day, if they can find wage labor, each of these pigs is worth 225 kina or more.

Members of the men's house group, the subclan section, and, to a lesser degree, the subclan expect food to be shared liberally and to be able to borrow tools or money when needed. Members of the subclan section refer to one another as brothers or sisters and interact, or are expected to interact, in a fashion consistent with that terminology.

"The solidarity of a group, quasi-group, or collectivity," according to Cohen (1968:135), "is a readiness to act in concert for certain purposes." It "may derive from interests which stem from internal social relations, or it may result from external pressures, or as is common, it may result from both." In terms of proximity of land holdings and residence, cooperation in gardening, house construction and ceremonial exchange and the willingness of groups to unite for common defense, the solidarity of the social groups that I have described is

*In earlier times, young boys played by shooting toy bows and arrows in prepara-
tion for their adult role in intergroup warfare. Here, on the ceremonial grounds
in front of the men's house, young boys shoot marbles instead of arrows. Some-
day, with luck and much effort, tribal warfare will no longer threaten life and
property, and boys won't need to practice the "art" of warfare.*

*In contrast to the men's house shown in the previous photo, which may house
forty to fifty men, married women live, with sons up to about age five and unmarried daughters, in individual houses built on land owned by their husbands.
Here Gunnabia, Council Sago's wife, sits in the doorway of her house.*

inversely related to their position in the segmentary hierarchy. The smaller the social distance (such as two members of the same section) the greater the sense of solidarity.

Brown (1970:99–100) notes that, for the Simbu, transactions between clans and tribe are competitive while those within a clan are reciprocal, leading to mutual assistance and support. Her discussion (1970:103) of the pattern of cooperation within the clan suggests that the greatest degree of mutual aid and cooperation is within a close group of patrilineal relatives and decreases as the social unit becomes more inclusive.

Other Relations

While the segmentary structure of tribe, clan, subclan, and subclan section provides the framework for intergroup relations and, therefore, provides guidelines for norms of behavior toward others, each individual is the center of a network of social relationships. The patrilineal structure divides an individual's biological kin into two groups. On the one hand, there are relatives descended through the male line, such as a person's father's brother's child (FBC). This person is, by birth, a member of his or her father's subclan section, which is the same as the father's brother's section and father's brother's child's section. The individual and his or her father's brother's child, whom we would call cousins, are members of the same subclan section. Anthropologists call this type of cousin a "parallel cousin" because the relationship is traced through siblings of the same gender. On the other hand, there are biological relatives who are not members of the patrilineal descent group. For example, a person's mother's brother's child, whom we would also call a cousin, is not a member of the clan. Why? Since members of a clan cannot marry, a person's parents must be from two different clans. The child is a member of his or her father's clan, not his or her mother's; therefore, the child is not a member of his or her mother's brother's clan or mother's brother's child's clan. Anthropologists call these "cross-cousins" (that is, a mother's brother's child, or a father's sister's child). What this means is that, in Simbu, all "cousins" are not alike. A person's father's brother's children are members of her or his patrilineal descent group, whereas the father's sister's children are not.

Marriage, I have noted, initiates and maintains mutually valuable relationships involving periodic gift exchanges and frequent assistance of various kinds. At the individual level, these relations cross-cut structural relations. In conflict situations, nonpatrilineal kin stress the importance of maintaining their highly valued relationship. Moreover, nonpatrilineal kin ties cross-cut hostile relations and relations of opposition between groups and, as Brown (1970a:100) points out, "Good relationships between affines lessens the likelihood of a dispute leading to a fight between groups." In a recent paper (Podolefsky 1984), I argued that the lower frequency of intertribal marriage in recent years has affected the ability of groups to contain conflict, and, as a result, tribal warfare emerged as a significant national problem in the 1970s.

LAND OWNERSHIP AND LAND USE

Land is the most important resource owned by the Simbu. Typically, slash-and-burn agriculturalists grow crops for shorter periods in years than they allow the land to lie fallow. In the core, high-population-density areas, the Simbu use complex and intensive agricultural techniques. In doing so, the Simbu are exchanging labor for land by making use of methods that permit permanent or semipermanent cultivation of a single area.

Throughout the Highlands, the length of the fallow period is correlated with the type of land ownership. Ownership falls into two broad types: individual rights in land and group rights in land. In low-density areas, land is owned by the kin group. Members of the group can use any land they wish. In high-density areas, men own land individually. In a survey of seventeen New Guinea Highland societies, Paula Brown and I (1976) found a perfect one-to-one correspondence between areas where gardens are under permanent or semipermanent cultivation (very short fallow period) and societies in which there are individual rights to land. We concluded that the type of land ownership might be considered a social concomitant of the length of the fallow period.

With the exception of men's houses and ceremonial ground sites, individuals own all the land that is part of the Kobulaku tribal territory and lies within the densely populated Marigl Valley. Moreover, individuals of other groups own all the land bordering the Kobulaku tribal territory on the east, west, and north. The southern portion of the tribal territory is forested bush. To reach this area, a person from Mul must traverse three mountains. This forested area is divided into four sections, each said to be owned by one of the original four clans. Any member of the clan may cut trees, plant gardens (and enclose them), or hunt in the section owned by his or her group, but such activities are forbidden to members of the other clans. The soil in this forest area is said to be fertile and sweet potatoes grown here are more highly valued than those grown in the densely populated areas where land is in frequent use.

Usually, people gain ownership of land through patrilineal inheritance. Before marriage, a young man relies on his mother, sisters, and his brothers' wives for food. They may give him a few banana trees or stands of sugar cane to care for and use as his own. When a man marries, his father allocates a portion of his land to his son. The young groom continues to live in the men's house while he constructs a house for his wife, usually either in the vicinity of his men's house or garden area. When a woman marries, she moves to her husband's group and grows most of her gardens on his land.

If a man has daughters, but no sons, he may loan parcels of land to their husbands. These loans may last over extended periods and eventually become permanent gifts if the husband resides with his father-in-law's group and participates in their activities. People recognize that this often leads to incorporating the couple's children into their mother's father's group, even though the children are not actually patrilineal descendents. They point out, however, that the present practice of census registration reminds people of their place of birth and makes it more difficult to maintain the fiction that the children are patrilineal descendents and have secure rights in the group. Upon his death a man's unallocated land is distributed among his sons and, sometimes, brothers.

People may also acquire land by simply planting a garden or building a house on it and waiting to see how upset the owner gets. This situation is exactly what set Sine and Gui against old Sago, whose son had just begun to build a house on Sine and Gui's land. Particularly along the borders, members of one group may gradually encroach into land of another. In this densely populated area, land is held tenaciously, and land encroachment may rapidly lead to intergroup fighting. Even brothers may fight over land that was not divided before their father's death.

Within a family, land is owned by the husband/father while most of the work is done by the female members of the family. Garden plots are dispersed in several areas and usually each family has more than one plot under cultivation at any given time. As a result, most families have alternative gardens available in the event that a pig damages one of them.

In initiating a garden, the man is responsible for clearing the ground of grass, scrub brush, and trees. He will also build a fence around the garden and till the soil with a digging stick. If the plot is within an area that will be enclosed by a group of men, they usually cooperate in fence construction. The grass and scrub brush are cut, turned until dried by the sun, and then burned. The owner of the ground then subdivides his plot, using rope and sticks for markers. If the garden is on a steep slope, some of these horizontal boundary markers will be reinforced to keep the soil from washing down the hill; sometimes ditches are dug along the horizontal to prevent erosion.

Most sections of the garden are used by the owner's wife. Some portions, however, may be lent to the owner's sisters, affines, or friends. After the burning of the trees and the initial tilling of the soil, gardening activities are taken over by women with only occasional help in weeding or fence repair by men. The women make the final preparation of the ground and plant yams and sweet potatoes in mounds approximately two feet in diameter. Gardens often include a mixture of leafy vegetables, cucumber, corn, winged beans, sweet potatoes (15 varieties), yams (16 varieties), and taro (10 varieties). Crops mature in approximately this order, and as a result, the gardens contain only sweet potatoes, yams, and taro after about four or five months from the time of planting. In the higher altitude gardens, onions and cabbage are frequently included in the place of taro and yams.

Throughout the area, people also plant and consume ten varieties of bananas, eight varieties of sugar cane, and four varieties of wild sugar cane with edible fruit known as *pitpit*. After the crops are harvested, pigs are put into the garden to root out remaining tubers. Typically, the garden will be replanted only in sweet potatoes. After two to four harvests, the ground lies fallow for three to five years, though a seven-year period is possible for those who have sufficient ground.

Beginning in 1959, the colonial administration introduced coffee as a cash crop. Only ten coffee trees were planted in 1959, but by 1965 there were 30,975 coffee trees in Mul (Patrol Report 1965). At the time, this was the largest number of coffee trees in any rest house area of the Gumine subdistrict. The administration introduced pyrethrum and passion fruit after coffee, but they did not provide comparable returns: pyrethrum because of the labor involved and passion fruit because of the low return and bulk of produce (Patrol Report 1971).

The introduction of cash crops is important in dispute settlement for two reasons. First, cash crops allow people to earn the money that is used in making compensation payments during the disputing process. People report that, in the past, they fought over such incidents as pigs breaking into gardens because they had nothing to pay compensation with. Second, the introduction of coffee has put additional pressures on land, particularly plots that are near the road, making the transport of the dried beans more economical.

Damage to gardens by pigs is an ever-present threat. With the exception of small piglets, pigs are seldom tethered as in the Central Simbu or fenced as in North America. After foraging freely during the day, they return home for an evening meal and are confined in some manner. Though this is the stated ideal, many people do not tie up their pigs unless a particular pig has had a history of damaging gardens. Even under these circumstances, pigs are not always adequately confined (see cases 4, 5, and 6). People say that pigs are both their pride and their agony.

CONCLUSION

In the previous chapter, I argued that the traditional ways of handling conflict had to be understood within the context of the culture and society as a whole. The purpose of this chapter has been to provide the background for that understanding. We have learned that the Simbu have only recently come into contact with the Western world. They are densely populated horticulturalists who grow sweet potatoes and other vegetables as their dietary staples. They raise pigs, but their primary use is for exchange during ceremonial events such as weddings. People do not raise their pigs for household food.

People define their individual relations and the relationships between their groups according to kinship principles and beliefs. The behavior expected between people and the importance of a relationship is defined by the groups to which people belong. As we begin to examine conflict, therefore, it is always important to concern ourselves not only with what the dispute is over but, even more importantly, whom it is between. The simplest form of conflict and conflict management is when it is between only two people—it is dyadic. We begin, therefore, with a look at dyadic conflict management processes among the Simbu.

Note

1. Since there exists a large body of literature concerning the Simbu (previously spelled Chimbu), I will not present a full ethnographic account here. Rather, I focus on those aspects of Simbu society particularly relevant to the study of law. Those interested in other aspects of traditional Simbu lifeways might wish to consult the following works: Aufenanger 1959; Brookfield 1973; Brookfield and Brown 1963; Brown 1960, 1961, 1962, 1963, 1964, 1966a, 1966b, 1967, 1969, 1970a, 1970b, 1972, 1974; Brown and Brookfield 1959, 1967; Brown and Winefield 1965; Criper 1968; Hatanaka 1972, 1973; Hide 1971, 1973, 1974; Howlett et al. 1976; Nilles 1950, 1953; Schafer 1938; Standish 1973.

3 / Conflict Management I:
Dyadic Processes

The behaviors of men and women are structured by the opportunities available to them. In any given society, there are a limited number of ways that individuals can reasonably react when they feel offended. In a conflict situation, people select among these options. Seldom do they go beyond the generally known and culturally accepted dispute processing mechanisms. Few Americans—virtually none—would resort to the supernatural, using divination to discover who had broken into their home and stolen the family silver. Neither would they consider calling a sorcerer to bring the thief to justice. Rather, they would call the police. In traditional Simbu society there were no police, so they could not consider that option. In this fashion an individual's behavior in a given conflict situation is limited by the *structure of opportunity* defined by his or her culture society.

The structure of opportunity for handling dispute cases in this New Guinea Highlands community consists of a range of options from avoidance to adjudication. These are linked in a complex pattern; a particular case may go through stages, making use of several of these options. In the case of the violent old men, for example, the initial response to a grievance was physical reprisal. Sine and Gui had been offended when Sago's son Koma began to build a house on their land, and they attacked old Sago. The three disputants went through an unsuccessful attempt at mediation, a trip to the police station at Gumine, and a second mediation session.

The goal of this book is to develop an understanding of conflict management in the context of Simbu culture and society. The first step in the analysis is to separately describe and examine each type of conflict management process. This lays the groundwork for an understanding of the larger system and the behavior of individuals within it.

TYPOLOGY OF CONFLICT MANAGEMENT

Classification is an important first step in any analysis. Unfortunately, social phenomena do not always lend themselves to unambiguous classification into discrete categories based on reasonably obvious and observable criteria. We have seen this problem in the historic debate over the definition of law discussed in the first chapter, and we could easily point to a variety of terms, such as "legal complexity," that are hard to define or measure (compare for example, Schwartz and Miller 1974; Newman 1983).

Klaus Koch (1974) and Philip Gulliver (1979) have each devised a six-category typology of dispute behavior. Koch refers to these as conflict management processes, while Gulliver describes his categories as "modes by which disputes are handled and resolution sought" (1979:1).

CLASSIFICATIONS OF CONFLICT MANAGEMENT BEHAVIOR

Koch (1974)	Gulliver (1979)
Avoidance	Avoidance
Coercion	Duels
Negotiation	Violent Self Help
Mediation	Appeal to Supernatural
Arbitration	Negotiation
Adjudication	Adjudication

No one can judge whether either of these classification schemes is inherently right or wrong based on objective criteria. They simply group the same phenomena in different ways. Most of the behaviors that Gulliver would categorize as duels, violent self help, or appeal to the supernatural, Koch would classify as coercion. Koch's categories of negotiation and mediation would be subsumed under Gulliver's category of negotiation. Similarly, Gulliver's definition of adjudication would include both Koch's categories of arbitration and adjudication. Sine and Gui's attack on old Sago would be classified as violent self help by Gulliver and as coercion by Koch.

Gulliver provides a graphic image of the distinction between negotiation and adjudication.

The picture of negotiation is one of two sets of people, the disputing parties or their representatives, facing each other across a table or from the opposite sides of an open space. They exchange information and opinion, engage in argument and discussion, and sooner or later propose offers and counter offers relating to the issues in dispute between them, seeking an outcome acceptable to both sides. The comparable picture of adjudication is that of two parties (each including one or more persons) who, separated from one another, face an adjudicator who sits in front of, apart from, and often raised above them. They address him. . . . Eventually the adjudicator pronounces his decision. . . .

. . . it is clear that a fundamental characteristic of negotiation is the absence of a third-party decision maker.

Gulliver's classification identifies three types of unilateral action: duels, violent self help, and appeal to the supernatural. The essential difference between adjudication and all of the other forms of conflict management, including negotiation, is the presence or absence of "an authoritative third party."

Koch's classification scheme pays less attention to differing types of coercion and greater attention to types of third-party intervention—mediation, arbitration, and adjudication. To envision mediation, picture Gulliver's two disputants facing each other across the negotiation table, but interject a third individual off to one side facing the two disputants. The disputants have not yet turned to address their arguments to a third party having the right and authority to impose a decision (as in adjudication), but neither are they any longer alone. The third party, while not empowered with the authority to make a decision, nevertheless facilitates the resolution of the conflict. For Koch the most salient feature concerns the transformation of a dyadic conflict between two parties into a triadic relationship between the two disputants and a third party intervener (mediator, arbitrator, or judge).

Figure 3-1 describes a variation of Koch's (1974:28) typology. The primary feature distinguishing conflict management process is the intervention of a third party. Dyadic processes involve direct interaction between the disputants, whereas triadic processes involve the intervention of a third party. Two types of third-party intervention are found in triadic processes, *ex officio* and mutual consent. In the first, a third party is officially charged with imposing himself or herself upon the dispute with or without the consent of the disputants. In the second type, the third party participates only with the consent of both disputants.

The second distinguishing feature is the type of outcome: authoritative judgment, bilateral agreement, unilateral imposition, or unilateral withdrawal. (Koch did not include this last category.) Authoritative judgment occurs where power is invested in an office (adjudication) or where the disputants agree to abide by the decision of the third party (arbitration). Bilateral agreement occurs both when the third party has no authority to impose a decision (mediation) and in the dyadic process of negotiation. Rather than coming to an agreement, one party may decide to take action without regard to the other party's concerns, as when Sine and Gui attacked old Sago. Therefore they unilaterally impose an outcome through coercion.

Finally, I have designated (in figure 3-1) the outcome associated with avoid-

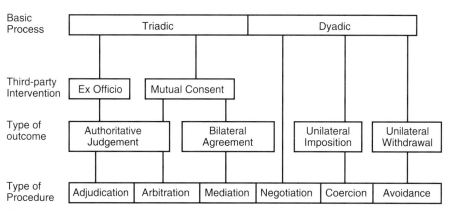

Figure 3-1   A Typology of Conflict Management

ance as "unilateral withdrawal" of a social relationship. In some cases, as we shall see, this withdrawal is intended to "punish" one's opponent, while in other cases the disputant is sufficiently powerless that he or she simply drops the issue and avoids the other party.

Different combinations of the dimensions of third-party intervention and type of outcome parsimoniously distinguish among six types of conflict management procedure: adjudication, arbitration, mediation, negotiation, coercion, and avoidance. Koch (1974:27–29) provides a series of definitions of these terms.

> In negotiation both principals seek a mutually acceptable settlement without the intervention of a third party but often with the aid of supporters.
>
> In mediation a third party intervenes in a dispute to help the principals achieve an agreement. Three modes of intervention are possible: either principal may solicit the mediator's aid, or an administrative agency may appoint the mediator, or the mediator may intervene on his own initiative as a party interested in conciliation of the conflict. . . .
>
> Adjudication demands the decision of a third party who has the official authority to render a judgement. Either principal may seek his intervention or he may exercise this role ex officio. The institutionalization of this process tends to formalize the norms of conduct and judicial procedure and requires means that enforce compliance with the decision.
>
> In arbitration both principals consent to the intervention of a third party whose judgement they agree to accept. . . .
>
> Through coercion one principal imposes the outcome and alone determines his concession, if any, to the opponent. The threat or use of force often aggravates the conflict and impedes a peaceful settlement. . . .
>
> Avoidance represents a procedure of indirect confrontation in which one principal takes no action to obtain redress for a wrong or a curtailment of his interests, although his withdrawal tactics may induce his opponent to make amends.

With the exception of arbitration, each of these types of conflict management processes is available to the people of Mul. In this chapter I describe the dyadic processes of avoidance, coercion, and negotiation. In the following chapter I examine the triadic processes of mediation and adjudication.

Avoidance

Simbu are contentious and tend to confront one another when aggrieved. While avoidance is always a potential, Simbu only occasionally use it as a way of inflicting harm. They are loathe to avoid an antagonist as a procedure of indirect conflict or even to allow a cooling off period. Rather, if no action is taken, it is generally because the offender is unknown; unavailable; or has been found, through previous direct interpersonal dealings with the aggrieved party, to be one who refuses to cooperate in seeking a solution.

There are exceptions, of course, and people do avoid one another as a result of conflict as the following case shows.

MEMORY CASE 1—BROTHERS QUARREL OVER LAND

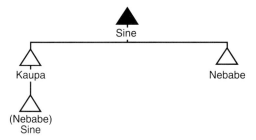

Sine

Kaupa   Nebabe

(Nebabe)
Sine

About twenty years ago Sine died without dividing his land between his two sons, Kaupa and Nebabe. Five years later Kaupa's first son was born. He named the boy Nebabe after his brother. He then planted a small coffee garden, which he said was to belong to his son when he grew older. Nebabe, the brother, apparently did not believe the land belonged to Kaupa. He demanded that Kaupa remove the trees and plant them elsewhere. The two brothers quarreled over the land and garden and eventually the ground was divided.

The brothers now live in different men's houses and have not spoken to each other for fifteen years. Kaupa went so far as to insist that his son's name be changed from Nebabe to Sine in the government census book.

In his typology of conflict management processes, Koch lists avoidance as a type of procedure with no outcome. This seems to me to be incorrect. *Avoidance involves the unilateral withdrawal of a social relationship.* The relationship may be highly valued or of no value at all. Breaking off relations may be done with great fanfare and publicity or it may be done quietly. Just as with coercion, or any other conflict management process, the effectiveness of the effort in a particular circumstance does not affect the definition of the process.

William Felsteiner (1974) describes communities in technologically complex rich societies as characterized by single-interest, low-value social relationships. The idea that avoidance has no outcome reflects this Western model of community. A typical scenario involves two neighbors in dispute over the dog or children. The conflict escalates until one of the parties opts out of the situation by moving to another apartment. Here avoidance would be the outcome. In many non-Western societies such mobility is difficult.

We can also envision scenarios in which avoidance is used with the same vicious intent as would be a club or knife, and with about the same subtlety. I am thinking of the small town in America where neighbors grow up and grow old among people they have known all their lives, the business executive with a long-term investment in the company, or the tenured school teacher or professor. In these situations, avoidance (or "not talking to") behavior is often public and intentional. When taken as an action against an offender, avoidance is intended to cause discomfort, bring about a loss of prestige, or exert pressure to force the opponent to reconsider an intransigent position. It may be intended as an instrument of retribution.

The Simbu case described above contains elements of both avoidance as an outcome ("lumping it") and as a procedure whose outcome is the unilateral withdrawal of a social relationship. Living in separate men's houses allowed each of the parties to opt out of an untenable position. Beyond this, Kaupa's insistence that his son's name be changed in the official village census book was a public attack on the status of his brother.

Coercion

Implicit or explicit, the threat of coercion is always present in conflict situations. The behavior exhibited by Sine and Gui has been repeated time and again throughout history in all parts of the world. From school yard squabbles to nuclear bombs, humans have exhibited an uncanny creativity in their ability to find new ways to coerce other humans. Even in negotiation it is better to argue from a position of strength than of weakness. And Sally Merry (1982) finds that effective mediators may coerce disputants into agreements. Can we distinguish coercion as a *type* of process from the use of coercion in other processes?

Of the types of conflict management procedures identified in Figure 3-1, coercion is most similar to avoidance. I could argue that in some instances avoidance is merely a particular strategy of coercion. From another perspective, coercion is sometimes a product of avoidance.

Where relationships are highly valued, the withdrawal of social relations is an indirect (and therefore often subtle) form of coercive power. Consider, for example, the situation of a man or woman who, over some affront, chooses not to speak with his or her spouse. On the other hand, where little value is placed on a relationship, avoidance is not particularly coercive, as in the case of someone who decides not to speak with the manager of a department store. The former is coercive, the latter is not.

In avoidance, the "coerciveness" of an action is directly related to the value of the social relationship existing between the disputants; avoidance may be coercive where relations are highly valued (or at least ongoing or face-to-face) but not coercive where relations are of little importance. Thus, coerciveness is a product of the relations between disputants, not of the avoidance behavior. This is not the case with the more direct sorts of behaviors usually included under the category of coercion. When one individual hits another over the head with a club, the victim bleeds regardless of the social relationship involved. *In coercion, "coerciveness" is a product of the act, not the relationship between the actors.*

Two forms of coercion are found in Mul. The first involves physical aggression directed against the offender. The second involves the use of the supernatural— witchcraft, divination, and sorcery.

Physical Aggression

In Mul, physical reprisals may be carried out against an offender's person or property, or, occasionally, though this was more common in the past, against the property or person of other members of the offender's kinship group. Violence is legitimized by its prominent place in traditional society, where older Simbu report that it was the most frequently used means of redressing a grievance. People believe that there is less violence today because of government attempts at pacification and because there are viable alternatives. Today, coercion is most commonly found in situations where the aggrieved party sees no other possible course of action.

Coercion comes in many forms in Mul. While the bows and featherless arrows of the Simbu are not particularly accurate at long distances, they are certainly fine for shooting a pig that has gone into a garden. The garden owner thus takes vengeance on the pig owner. Anger can also be expressed by ripping out an antagonist's coffee or pandanus trees or physically attacking the offender (or one of his or her kin).

Although violence is frequent in the New Guinea Highlands, there are significant constraints. The use of coercion invariably precipitates a new grievance. The notion of "just deserts"—they got what they deserved—does not excuse coercive behavior, and, as I will discuss later, compensation must be paid for all injury.

While there are structural and situational determinants that tend to lead to the use of coercion, in any society there are individuals, if not categories of people, who are more prone to violence than the majority of the population. I was often told that the older men who grew up before contact with Europeans behave in the "fashion of their grandparents" and are more frequently violent. We have already seen this is the case of Sine and Gui's attack on old Sago.

Witchcraft, Divination, and Sorcery

Another mechanism of coercion, associated more with the past than the present, is the appeal to the supernatural: witchcraft, divination, and sorcery. According to anthropological definition, witchcraft is an inherent quality where divination and sorcery are learned. Witches use no rites, no spells, and no medicines—witchcraft is a psychic act. Sorcerers use magic rites with bad medicines. Divination is a method of discovering what is unknown and often what cannot be known, by experiment and logic (Evans-Pritchard 1937).

The study of these features of Highland social life has focused primarily on accusations rather than acts of witchcraft or sorcery. Moreover, the focus has been on the role sorcery plays in maintaining the solidarity of the social group. For societies with stable local organizations, that is, permanently settled descent groups, as in Mul, the hypothesis has been advanced that these societies, "in the absence of wars for territorial or other economic aggrandizement, can preserve their identity only by mutual suspicion, rivalry, and hostility. Sorcery accusations act here both as an important medium for expressing enmity and as an excuse for initiating warfare, which is ultimately the most effective means of relieving feelings of aggression" (Lawrence and Meggitt 1965:17). In some cases, such as the Kainantu peoples, the rate of sorcery has risen since the administration banned warfare. The warlike Mae Enga, in contrast, were little interested in sorcery and have not developed it since pacification. The difference is attributed to the existence of alternative means of channeling aggression and to the Mae's preference for the use of the Administration's Court of Native Affairs rather than traditional processes for settling disputes (Lawrence and Meggitt 1965:18).

David Hayano (1973) revealed that sorcery accusations were not randomly distributed among the Tauna Awa. He found that as physical distance increases, rates of social interaction, including sorcery accusations, decrease. And, secondly, that sorcery accusations "tend to be projected more often on those groups of individuals who are perceived to be more dissimilar and negatively stereotyped" (Hayano 1973:181). This distribution reinforces the notion that sorcery accusations help small autonomous sociopolitical units maintain their identity.

In a discussion of the killing of five accused male witches, Reay (1976) notes that the killing or banishment of an individual is, among the Kuma, a demonstration of social solidarity; it expresses the welfare of the group over that of the individual. Reay (1976:8) also reports that "a Kuma looks for witches among people he dislikes, but when he finds one there no one believes him." Many of the witchcraft accusations coincide with old grudges, and she implies that the community, seeing through the accuser's motives, ignores the accusation. In a similar light, Lindenbaum (1971:284) points out that "Sorcery accusations do not appear to be mechanisms of social control, rather sorcery beliefs operate as an expression of present political reality." (see also Berndt 1962:220)

In these works, the focus is on sorcery accusations rather than sorcery itself. It is the public accusation which draws a group together in opposition to its accused attacker. *Accusations* are not mechanisms of social control, as Lindenbaum points out. But what of sorcery itself? Little has been written on the use of supernatural agents in New Guinea as a response to a grievance.

In her treatment of Kuru sorcery among the Fore, Lindenbaum (1979:58) notes:

> All the maladies Fore consider significant require a judgment as to cause, which always involves some sort of socially disapproved act, although the ascription of guilt differs for each category. Sorcery results from the deliberate activities of politically hostile outsiders, of enemies in another parish or parish section, who must be exposed by divination or threat. The responsibility for lesser ailments falls within the parish section, the minimal political unit, where the offense is patent and does not require detection. These minor illnesses derive from some wrongdoing by the victim or close kinsperson, and involve the relationship of a person on his or her group's land, to people who have recently been members of the group, or to present residents. Sorcery allegations thus appear to be statements about political relations with other groups, whereas interpretations of other ailments refer to personal relations, rules of behavior, property rights, and common responsibilities within the group itself. These involve issues common to legal systems everywhere: the proper definition of murder, manslaughter, negligence, and accident.

Sorcery is not necessarily the initial act in a conflict. Sorcery, in fact, may be the New Guinean version of the "long arm of the law." Lindenbaum (1979:120) finds that "Sorcerers are the aggrieved, out to settle debts. . . . Thus, adulterers who take runaway wives expect retaliation from the abused husband, while great fighters think of sorcerers arising from the ranks of the unavenged. . . . Men rail at the presence of sorcerers, yet in a sense the sorcerer's motives are understandable. Reciprocal aggression is an outgrowth of prior victimization" (Lindenbaum 1979:125).

Witchcraft in Mul

In Mul, witchcraft is thought to be used only by women. The Pidgin English term *sanguma* is used to refer to the creatures women use to carry out their nefarious tasks as well as the spirits who roam the paths at night. I was told that in the past each woman had her own *sanguma* but that today many young women do not. No contradiction is seen between this and the belief that a witch's powers are passed through the blood in the female line. If a mother had a *sanguma,* so will her daughter—she cannot rid herself of it.

Simbu believe that *sanguma* are dogs, rats, bats, snakes, or other creatures that reside in the witch's stomach. Women are able to speak to these *sanguma* and order them to kill any man, woman, or child, by day or night. Emphasis is usually placed on the death of males. Some believe that the *sanguma* must ask the woman for permission to eat a particular person. If she allows it, it will go, but if she says no, then the *sanguma* cannot leave her stomach. Sometimes, according to informants, the *sanguma* only makes its victims sick, but other times it "eats his liver" and death follows immediately. "Men do not realize what is happening to them, they just feel ill and die," reported one of the older men.

If a woman who comes from another group, particularly another tribe, is believed to have killed a man by witchcraft, the victim's group will be upset with the witch's group, but it is said that this did not usually result in intergroup fighting. However, fear of witchcraft attacks from women prevented intermarriage with opposing groups during hostilities.

One man complained about the ban on killing witches since the arrival of Europeans. He reported that they had tried bringing witches to the government court but that the Europeans did not believe their accusations. "Now," he said, "women can just go around killing people."

He reported that in the past, they have dealt with witches by tying a black rope around their necks and throwing them into the Marigl River to drown. Accused witches often pointed out others as responsible, or as accomplices, and several might be killed. This sometimes led to fights between the witch's husband and his own group who killed her.

Despite this belief, there were, to my knowledge, no accusations of witchcraft during my stay in Mul. The following case occurred in August 1976, a few months before I arrived. It was reported to me independently on several occasions.

MEMORY CASE 2—THE SCHOOLBOY'S DEATH

A member of the Malaku clan had completed his schooling at Gumine and was attending high school at Kerowagi. Since he was one of the first to achieve this degree of schooling, it was believed that in the future he would be a highly valuable community member. During August he returned to Mul to spend a month with his relatives. Three days after he had returned to school he died. The men say that the doctor at Kerowagi told them that he had cut the boy open and found his liver to have been eaten (if he did say such a thing he most likely did not intend it to be understood to mean that it was a result of witchcraft).

Ten of the boys classificatory mothers were accused of using witchcraft. Ropes were placed around their necks and they were hoisted up into the trees. The women at first denied the charge, but eventually they admitted that the boy had stolen a taro from them and they became angry so they ate his insides. One said she had a dog in her stomach. They asked where she had gotten it and she replied that her mother had given it to her. When asked where it was now, she answered that when the men tied her up it ran away into the bush. She told them that she had not killed the boy, the dog had. A second woman said that her *sanguma* was a snake, but her snake had not killed the boy. The third woman also had a snake, the fourth a cassowary, the fifth a dog, the sixth a rat, the seventh a rat, the eighth a pig, the ninth a horse, and the tenth a cow. (The latter two animals are not native to New Guinea.) They told the men that when they want to kill a man they join together. They also said they were able to bring men up out of the grave, whereupon they take them into the bush, cut them up like pigs, and give the parts to their friends. Each woman then eats a bit of the body.

The women were neither killed nor banished from the area.

The fact that this story is repeated in this fashion does not mean that all the details are accurate. Nonetheless, it does outline some basic beliefs about the existence of witchcraft. An admission of witchcraft made under duress certainly does not prove that the women actually believed themselves to be witches. Witches, as the people of Mul conceive them, certainly cannot exist. The crucial question, for our purposes, is whether or not women, past or present, believe that they have these *sanguma* and make use of them as a response to a grievance, as was described in the above case. It is possible that each woman believes that there are witches within the tribe but that she herself received no *sanguma* from her mother and, therefore, is not a witch. This would result in the absence of people who believe themselves to be witches despite the generalized belief that witches do exist.

At this point, I have no evidence that any woman, at any given time, believes herself to be a witch and consciously makes use of her *sanguma* to redress a grievance. At the same time, people believe that witchcraft can be used by women to redress grievances.

Divination and Sorcery

Divination and sorcery are linked, in Mul, in that both require recourse to a man of special knowledge who manipulates objects to obtain desired ends. I was told that divination and sorcery had been used in precontact times but that there never were many specialists and their knowledge was not comparable to that of the people to the south in the Bomai and Karimui areas.

At the time of my fieldwork, there was only one man in the entire Kobulaku tribe who possessed this knowledge. People were not certain why he was the only one nor where he had learned how to use divination and sorcery. They believe he may have learned it in "Goroka or Karimui, or somewhere." Anyone could avail themselves of his services—for a fee.

Divination is used only in cases of theft where previous natural methods of detection (such as following footprints) have failed. In the past, the victim of a theft might put bamboo spikes around the base of a tree so that he or she would be able to follow the bloody tracks of the next thief. Although "man-traps" have been made illegal, divination has not become more frequent as a result.

The divination procedure involves bringing an object that has been associated with the stolen item, such as part of a banana tree in the case of stolen bananas, to the diviner, who places it on one end of a bamboo tube. This tube is prepared in advance by drilling a small hole about halfway up. The diviner then calls out names. When the name of the guilty party is mentioned, an insect is said to crawl up the bamboo tube and into the hole. Everyone then knows the identity of the perpetrator and the victim is able to confront the accused.

In the only case of divination reported to me during my stay in Mul, two men were accused of stealing bananas. They denied the charge and the issue was dropped. I was never able to learn exactly why no further action was taken. During my stay in Mul, there were, to my knowledge, no acts of sorcery and no sorcery accusations. I was told that following divination, the bamboo tube could be used by the sorcerer to make the accused person sick, die, or at least have an accident. The object associated with the stolen item is placed, along with a special leaf, inside the bamboo tube. The opening is sealed with dirt and the tube is heated in a fire. After the tube gets tight from the heat, it "explodes." Shortly afterward the thief's stomach swells up, and he or she dies. An alternate technique is to hold up the bamboo tube and a chicken, call out the name of the thief and kill the chicken. That night, people believe, the culprit will have diarrhea and die. People described several variations on this theme.

A few months into our stay in Mul, we arranged a trip to a mission where we could purchase some laying hens that would, in a couple of weeks, begin to provide us with some of the fresh protein we sorely craved. Canned mutton gets tiresome after a very short while. One morning we awoke to find that two of our hens had been stolen. Looking back on it now, it seems almost comical, but at the time the hens represented a nearly irreplaceable protein source, and one that provided a mental link to things more familiar. During the day, friends dropped by and commiserated with us on our loss. We looked for footprints or other ways to trace the culprit. I even went so far as to run a string from the gate of our little chicken coop through the bamboo walls of our house and to a tin can with a nail inside, which would function like an alarm bell. One friend suggested we should use divination. The use of an all-knowing detective (divination) to find the culprit, and the use of a means of punishment that finds the perpetrator wherever he or she may be (sorcery) seemed, at first, pretty efficient. It was then that I began to explore more carefully the ramifications of the use of the supernatural.

It became clear that if someone becomes ill or dies because of sorcery, the person who paid the sorcerer is responsible for paying compensation to the victim of the sorcery. Notions of justice do not eliminate the necessity of compensation for injury. Thus, while sorcery is an option for pursuing a grievance, there are considerable constraints against its use. I, for one, was not going to take the chance that someone might think I was responsible for another's illness or death, so I didn't use divination or sorcery to find the thief who stole my chickens.

The *threat* of sorcery may also be employed as a response to a grievance, as the following case shows.

CASE 1—THE CASE OF THE STOLEN PANDANUS FRUIT

On the night of February 8, 1977, three oil pandanus fruit were stolen from the garden of Council Sago. To the young people the oil pandanus fruit is just a vegetable, but, as Council Sago explained, to the older men like himself "it is their blood." Moreover, these particular fruits were large ones that Council Sago had been planning to use as part of a ceremonial gift to be given two weeks later. The occasion was part of a series of exchanges initiated a few months earlier by the marriage of a Naraku man to an Egaku woman and, as the councilor of the Naraku clan, Sago was to play a prominent role in the ceremonies.

Residents near the government station, who seemed quite concerned, reported that the councilor had come to the small market at the station and announced that if his pandanus were not returned the following day, he would use sorcery to make the thief die.

That night, Sago had a good laugh while I inquired about his behavior at the market. He said that he was just walking around and letting people know what had happened, hoping that maybe, if they were ashamed, they would return his pandanus fruit. As far as sorcery goes, he said that he did not know any; "You need a special man," he said. He also emphasized that, as a councilor, he would not be setting a good example if he used sorcery. Furthermore, he noted emphatically that if he did use sorcery and someone died as a result, he would have to make a large compensation payment.

Negotiation

Negotiation involves bilateral, rather than unilateral, action. By this I mean two individuals or groups jointly participating in the conflict management process rather than one taking unilateral action against the other. The transformation from unilateral to bilateral action—the laying down of arms and the decision to come to terms with an opponent—is probably the most important breakthrough in a grievance situation. Such a decision, in a generic sense, must precede the transformation from a dyadic to triadic process. Indeed, at times negotiation is a stage that precedes the use of a triadic process. Negotiation may also be used when the issue is too trivial to involve a third party.

Most often, however, the use of negotiation presents a message distinct from unilateral and triadic processes. The message is that the relationship is more important than the grievance, and that the disputants would like, if possible, to come to agreement without the intervention of others.

We negotiate all the time. We negotiate with friends, husbands or wives, kin, colleagues, and strangers. We negotiate with friends (including spouses) about what movie to see on a Saturday night, and we negotiate the exchange of a garment with a store manager. Negotiation is clearly different from violence and sorcery on the one hand and adjudication on the other.

Negotiation is defined by characteristics of the process, not the tone of voice or the place of discussion. In Mul, as in America, negotiations may be loud and hostile or subdued and amicable. They occur in public places such as the ceremonial ground or on the road, in the semiprivacy of a garden path or men's house, or in the privacy of a garden or woman's house.

The following case is not untypical of a negotiated settlement.

CASE 2—A FRIENDLY DISPUTE OVER DAMAGE

Members of the same clan, as mentioned earlier, sometimes enclose several gardens within the same fenced area to conserve the wood and labor required for building fences. Koma, old Sago's oldest son, (Naraku clan) owned a garden at the top of one such enclosure. The land below Koma's belonged to Yoba (Naraku clan). This particular year Yoba had decided to loan some garden land to his friend Adolip (Kunaraku clan).

Although the land was loaned by Koma to his friend Adolip and the garden was referred to as Adolip's, most of the gardening was done by Adolip's wife. Although the garden is said to belong to men, women do the daily garden work and, in fact, have much to say in such cases.

The arrangement was that Adolip (actually his wife) could garden the land for a year but Yoba retained all rights of ownership.

One night in April, four pigs broke into Adolip's garden and caused serious damage by eating the vegetables that were growing there. One of the pigs belonged to Kai. Two of the pigs were not seen and therefore their ownership was unknown. Adolip believed that the fourth pig belonged to Koma but that he had taken it out of the garden before anyone could see it. Koma, however, denied the charge.

Koma was a man with great potential for violence. When his father, old Sago, was beaten, he challenged the attackers to do battle with him instead. While this dispute was only over garden crops, readers unfamiliar with New Guinea societies, or subsistence economies in general, should keep in mind that the loss of crops creates a very serious problem. People cannot simply go to the local supermarket to replace their lost food. With luck they will have enough from other gardens. If not, they will have to borrow from others in the community. Thus, the stage was set for a potentially serious conflict over the damaged vegetables.

The morning after the event Koma met with Adolip at the latter's "men's" house. By singing out across the mountains to others who relayed the message far and wide, Koma summoned Kai and any others whose pig had caused the damage. We waited over an hour for Kai. In cases such as this, where community interest and emotional concern are not high, there is little social pressure on disputants and there is no one with the authority to order someone to respond when summoned.

Eventually Kai appeared, and we moved to a place under a shady tree where the men began to discuss what had transpired. Adolip explained to the others that his wife had told him to accept no less than twenty kina (about U.S. $26.00) for the ruined vegetables. Moreover, she had told him that if they offer only ten or fifteen kina he should tell them to forget it and wait until she returned from Omkalai (a walk of several hours). (Twenty kina was, according to my field assistant, a fair estimate of the value of the damaged food).

After brief discussion, Koma gave six kina to Adolip and said he would get the rest later. At this point I gave Koma four kina, which he passed on to Adolip. (That afternoon Koma returned the four kina to me.) Kai gave four kina and said he would give Adolip another six kina later. Thus the case ended as it had begun—amicably.

CONCLUSION

Every society affords its members a range of options for pursuing a grievance. The first step in the analysis of a conflict management system is to identify and describe each of the dispute-handling procedures which, collectively, form the *structure of opportunity*. To organize these dispute events, I used a variation of Klaus Koch's typology of conflict management procedures. This typology identifies six categories of conflict management procedure: avoidance, coercion, negotiation, mediation, arbitration, and adjudication. These can be compared and contrasted on the dimensions of third-party intervention and type of outcome.

The second part of the chapter focused on the dyadic process of conflict management, namely, those that do not make use of a third party. I found that avoidance, coercion, and negotiation are all options open to Mul residents. Coercion, whether violence or the use of the supernatural, generally precipitates a new grievance and leads to the expansion rather than the containment of the conflict. Negotiation, while a dyadic process, is fundamental in that it represents a stage in which individuals and groups talk out their conflict. The problem of "getting them to the table" is essentially one of rejecting avoidance and coercion and proceeding through negotiation or some third-party process. Mediation, as we shall see in the next chapter, introduces the notion of third-party intervention.

4 / Conflict Management II:
Triadic Processes

The intervention of a third party into the conflictual relationship between two disputants transforms the process from dyadic to triadic. A teacher comes between two quarreling students. Children seek out a friend or parent. Husband and wife go to a friend, a minister, or a marriage counselor. A victim and assailant come before a judge. And the leaders of Israel and Egypt meet with an American president at Camp David. All of these involve a third party attempting to help the disputants resolve their difficulties. In some instances, the third party has influence but no formal authority. In others, the third party has the authority to impose a fine or jail sentence.

Traditional societies of New Guinea did not produce highly developed triadic dispute-handling mechanisms. There were no formal agents of social control: no police, no courts, and no correctional institutions. There were no persons with the authority to render judgments or unilaterally impose socially legitimate sanctions. Did triadic forms of dispute processing exist in the Highlands? Or were intragroup relations characterized by a Hobbesian war of all against all?

Descriptions of dispute handling gleaned from the ethnographic literature suggest that there was relative uniformity across the Highlands in processes using third-party intervention. However, while procedural law shows some consistency, less is known about substantive law (Scaglion 1983). In an earlier study (Podolefsky 1987), I compared fifteen Highlands societies, revealing that in the precontact and early postcontact periods there were restrictions on warfare within particular groups. Within these smaller units there were means, though vaguely defined, by which disputes could be resolved without resort to violence.

Throughout the Highlands the individual or individuals who felt wronged initiated dispute resolution processes. Whether brought to public notice or handled more privately, cases remained disputes between individuals or groups rather than being transformed into offenses against society. Public dispute process often involved the use of a third-party intervener. This was not an office, but rather a role which was not highly differentiated from other leadership roles. Anthropologists have generally described the third party as an arbitrator or mediator rather than an adjudicator. Mediation is the best term to characterize the process since the intervener was not, typically, empowered with the authority to impose sanctions nor was he (it was always a male) a strong force in arriving at a settlement. Most descriptions suggest that the mediator listened passively, interjecting only to clarify a point, until he recognized the sense of community sentiment, at which point he urged disputants to come to an agreement.

At the time of my fieldwork, however, Simbu could choose between adjudication in the official court system or unofficial and informal mediation in local moots. In other areas of Papua New Guinea, *Village Courts* were being introduced. These Village Courts provide a middle ground between traditional conflict management and adjudication in introduced courts (Scaglion 1985; Westermark 1981). None were located in the vicinity of Gumine or Mul during this time.

This chapter describes two forms of triadic dispute handling available to the people of Mul—mediation through local moots and adjudication in the official court available at the government station.

OFFICIAL COURTS

The official legal system in use in Papua New Guinea follows the Australian model. The highest court is the Supreme Court, followed by the District Court and the Local Court. The law introduced was primarily English common law. The distinction between criminal and civil law has been maintained and, although both types of cases are heard by the same courts, the rules of procedure and evidence are somewhat different. For criminal offenses, the Queensland Criminal Code was adopted wholesale. This is justified by early administrators' claims that there was no readily identifiable preexisting alternative (Barnett 1972:61). S. H. Johnson (1969:101) states that before Europeans came to Papua New Guinea, there had been no system of public justice and little in the nature of communal punishment of crime. These statements reflect the prevailing attitude that legitimated the wholesale imposition of an alien legal system on the traditional cultures of Papua New Guinea.

On December 23, 1974, the Papua New Guinea Criminal Code came into being, and on January 11, 1975, it was put into operation, displacing the Queensland Code. The new code is modeled on the earlier one and neither provide for the consideration of native customary law.

Until 1966, cases involving Europeans were heard in the official court system, which did not yet include local courts, while cases involving indigenes were heard in courts of native affairs presided over by government patrol officers. A special set of simply-defined regulations prohibited minor criminal offenses, such as theft and fighting, and "administrative offenses," including refusal to follow a patrol officer's orders, or violations of census regulations or hygiene rules (Barnett 1972:60–61). In civil disputes, these courts "were expected to do justice and to encourage harmonious and peaceful settlement" (Barnett 1972:60–61). In New Guinea, as opposed to Papua, formal recognition was given to native customs, save when they were repugnant to the general principals of humanity (Barnett 1972b:618).

Law enforcement is guided by the *Native Customs' (Recognition) Ordinance* 1963, which requires all courts to take account of native customs in civil cases involving land (or rights to rivers and seas), marriage, divorce, child custody, trespass by animals, and transactions intended by parties to be governed by custom or where the court considers that by not taking custom into account, injustice will or may be done to a person. Native custom is not taken into account in a criminal case except for ascertaining the defendant's state of mind or for deciding upon the reasonableness of an act, default, omission, or excuse. Custom may also be considered when deciding whether to convict a guilty party and in determining the penalty to be imposed.

The local court is the only one that sits regularly at the Gumine government station; it is, therefore, the only one of the three levels of official courts relevant to the study of dispute handling in Mul.

Local Courts

The Local Court has jurisdiction over all offenses of the law of the territory that may be dealt with summarily (i.e., without a jury), civil actions, native matters arising out of custom (except those within the exclusive jurisdiction of the Lands Titles Commission), and any contravention of Local Government Council rules. Any party may elect to have matters dealt with by the District Court rather than the Local Court if he or she so chooses (*Local Court Act* 1963–1966).

In civil matters the Local Court is empowered to award damages or compensation, order restitution or the return of property, order the specific performance of a contract other than a contract for service, or make any other order that justice requires. The value of damages or compensation ordered cannot exceed K 200.00 (approximately U.S. $260). The complainant cannot divide the cause of action to make two or more complaints, though he or she may abandon the excess so that the case may be heard in the Local Court. The court is also empowered to grant a certificate that a marriage has been dissolved if the parties were married according to native custom.

A Local Court magistrate may mediate in a civil matter at any stage or before the hearing with a view to the just and amicable settlement. The magistrate may also postpone a hearing if he or she thinks the parties may be able to settle it themselves. Once a negotiated or mediated settlement is reached, it may be embodied in an official decision without further hearing.

In criminal cases, the local court is empowered to order a fine not exceeding K 100.00 (approximately U.S. $130) or sentence the defendant to a term of imprisonment not to exceed six months. The court may also order additional payment of compensation up to K 200.00 as the justice of the case requires. Fines may be paid in installments. In default of payment of the fine, the court may order imprisonment subject to the following scale.

TABLE 4-1   PRISON SENTENCE EQUIVALENTS

Fine (in kina)*	Maximum Sentence
K 4–10	1 month hard labor
10–30	2 months hard labor
30–50	3 months hard labor
50–70	4 months hard labor
70–90	5 months hard labor
90+	6 months hard labor
200+	12 months hard labor (District Court)

*K 1.00 = approx. U.S. $1.30

During civil cases, both parties to the dispute should be present and the complaint should be read out loud and explained in a language the defendant can understand. The defendant must be advised that he or she has the right to have the case heard in District Court and is not obliged to make any defense before the Local Court. If the defendant does not admit the complaint, the court first hears the evidence of the complainant followed by the witnesses for the complainant, then proceeds to hear the evidence of the defendant followed by witnesses. After each party has given evidence, the opposing party is entitled to cross-examine. The magistrate may ask questions at any stage of the proceedings, and the court may recall the parties or witnesses at any time. After hearing all the evidence, the court considers a verdict, which is pronounced in open court.

The procedure in the criminal court is essentially the same except that it is the prosecutor, rather than the complainant, who brings witnesses and gives evidence. The defendant is not required to testify or to give evidence (*Local Court Act 1963–1966*).

THE GUMINE LOCAL COURT
AND ITS RELEVANCE TO MUL

The courthouse is the largest building on the Gumine government station, three miles west of Mul. The rectangular building is constructed of tree trunks stripped of their bark. The high roof is thatched with sword grass. On the sides, walls of woven mats enclose only the lower four feet, allowing onlookers to peer curiously into the courtroom and observe the hearings taking place inside. In this way, people learn about the law of the government. During criminal cases, only defendants and officials are allowed inside the courtroom, while victims must stand outside among the crowd of interested onlookers.

At one end of the building is the magistrate's office, where court records are kept. Inside the courtroom, adjacent to his office, the magistrate sits behind a large desk. Opposite is a table and chair reserved for the prosecutor, who attends court in a police uniform. To the prosecutor's left is the witness box. Since the magistrate assigned to the court during my stay was from Goroka and did not understand the Simbu languages, a translator was positioned between the magistrate and the witness box. There are no other furnishings. In the rear of the courtroom, a police officer and the defendants awaiting trial stand or sit on the bare earthen floor.

Given the entirely alien and unfamiliar scene, it is hardly surprising that local residents appear ill at ease when brought into the courtroom, either as defendant witness. People seem much more relaxed during informal mediations in the magistrate's office. It is clear that despite the best efforts of police and the magistrate, local residents do not fully comprehend the official legal system or their rights under it. People are even less familiar with the District Courts, which sit at the provincial capital, and are quite unlikely, therefore, to exercise their right to have cases heard before that court.

During the 1976 calendar year, 490 cases were brought to the criminal sector of the Gumine Local Court. Table 4-2 summarizes the types and frequencies of these cases. Most striking is the large proportion of cases that have no basis in traditional society. Riotous behavior and possession of weapons would certainly have occurred in the precontact era but would not, in and of themselves, have resulted in a dispute case. Not paying taxes, betting, escape, and a variety of motor vehicle offenses are but a few examples of offenses that have no history in the community. Many of these cases reflect events occurring on or around the government station or involving station personnel.

TABLE 4-2   CRIMINAL OFFENSES: GUMINE LOCAL COURT—1976

	N	%
Behaving in a riotous manner	138	28.0
Failure to pay local government tax	71	14.5
Theft	49	10.0
Unlawful striking/Use of violence	44	8.9
Betting/Playing an unlawful game	43	8.7
Possession of offensive weapon	19	3.8
Trespass	12	2.4
Unlawfully laying hold	12	2.4
Escape (or attempted) from police	11	2.2
Drinking on a moving vehicle	10	2.0
Adultery	9	1.8
Behaving in a threatening manner	8	1.6
Property damage	7	1.4
Spreading false reports	6	1.2
Insulting or offensive behavior	6	1.2
Drunk and disorderly in public	6	1.2
Driving without a license	6	1.2
Entering motor vehicle without consent	6	1.2
Obscene language	5	1.0
Possession of stolen property	3	0.6
Driving negligently	3	0.6
Driving administrator's car without consent	3	0.6
Failure to share local government work	3	0.6
Failure to give information to police	2	0.4
Resisting arrest	2	0.4
Selling liquor without a license	2	0.4
Driving while drinking	2	0.4
Interfering with a motor vehicle	2	0.4
Unregistered motor vehicle	1	0.2
Uninsured motor vehicle	1	0.2
Contravening direction by police	1	0.2
Obstructing the police in their duty	1	0.2
Giving false name/address to police	1	0.2
Possession of a police uniform	1	0.2
Debt (pig)	1	0.2
Urinating in public	1	0.2
Use of an unregistered firearm	1	0.2
Use of a used postage stamp	1	0.2
Total Cases	490	100.0

In 148 of the 490 cases, the defendant was found guilty and fines were ordered. In *every case,* however, the defendant elected to default on the payment and serve an equivalent prison term (see table 4-1) instead. Only ten cases (2%) were referred to the District Court. Five of these involved persons who were charged with trespass, obscene language, and driving the administrator's car without his consent. These were not local-level disputes, nor were the accused local community members. Rather, these were government personnel who had come from other areas and who were far more knowledgeable about dealing with government agencies than were the local community members.

Most civil matters that are brought to the Local Court are handled by the magistrate during informal mediation sessions in his office and no formal court records are kept. The civil court register of the Local Court shows only thirty-six cases for the 1976 calendar year. Twenty-seven (75%) of these were crossed out, indicating that they were not heard by the magistrate.

Six of the nine (67%) civil cases that were heard in open court were brought by husbands whose wives had deserted them. In three of these cases the wife was ordered to return to her husband. In two cases the magistrate order the relatives to return the husband's bride price. And in one case the couple agreed to remarry. Of the three nonmarital cases, two involved debt. One of these concerned the debt of a pig and the other concerned two bags of sweet potatoes. In the former case, the wrong defendant appeared and the case was dismissed. In the latter case a payment of six kina was ordered. In the last of the nine civil cases, five men were charged with removing parts from a motor vehicle. Only two appeared before the court and they were ordered to pay K50.00. An order was issued that the others should pay the same within two months.

If one begins a study in a local community rather than with court records, one gets a very different picture of the court use. The court at Gumine draws its case load from diverse areas surrounding the government station. But only certain types of cases reach the court.

During my stay, I recorded sixty-five dispute cases in Mul. Of the sixty-five cases, only six were taken out of the community to the government station. In each case this occurred because the local remedy agents were unable to bring about a settlement. When this happens, disputants walk to the government station, where the first stop is the police station. The police officers act as gatekeepers, using their discretion regarding how they think cases should be handled. The police can discourage disputants by telling them that, if they proceed to court, someone will end up in jail and that it is a terrible place where people, particularly older people, may die.

Four of the six cases brought to the government station did not get past the police. Two cases were dropped by the disputants and two others were sent back to be mediated at the local level. In one case the police directed the disputants to the magistrate for informal mediation. He suggested that locals mediate.

Only one of the sixty-five cases was heard in the official court system. Thus, only a very small proportion (1.5%) of the cases that began in the local community wound up in the official courts and were recorded in the official court records.

Similarly, Scaglion (1985:94) found that among the Abelam of the Sepik area (who have a longer history of contact than do Simbu), about 5 percent of all conflict cases that arose in the village ended up in Local Court.

These findings have very obvious implications for the study of conflict in the Highlands. First, Local Court records are not a representative sample of conflict or dispute cases in Highlands communities. Second, most conflict is handled within the local community. This most frequently occurs in informal mediations (or moots) that are referred to in pidgin as *kots*.

MEDIATION

There is little doubt that the most frequently used means of handling grievances publicly is through mediation by local government councilors and their assistants *(komitis)*. These procedures, referred to by the pidgin term *kot* (court), have been called "unofficial courts" by Strathern (1972a, 1972b) since they are not recognized by the Papua New Guinea government and "moots" by Scaglion (1981), following the tradition of legal anthropology.

To understand the role played by the councilors and *komitis* we need to look briefly at the historical development and contemporary legitimacy of the moot. It appears that the legitimacy of the unofficial courts stems from three sources: (a) the early contact experience and the historical development of the moot; (b) the necessity for a readily available means of handling the day-to-day conflicts that arise in the community without resorting to violence, a strategy which had been prohibited by the colonial government; and (c) the contemporary reinforcement of the system by police, government administrators, and magistrates.

During the early contact period of the 1950s, *luluais* and *tultuls* were appointed by government patrol officers *(kiaps)*.

> The duties of a luluai may be thus summarized: He acts as the representative of the Administration in his village, and sees that all orders and regulations are observed. He is responsible for maintaining good order, and he reports promptly to the Administration any breach of the peace or irregularity that may occur. He adjudicates in quarrels and minor matters of difference among the people. . . .
>
> The tultul's duties are to convey to the people any orders or information received by the luluai from the Administration. He is simply a means of communication between those in authority and the people. . . .
>
> The principal element in the bringing of a village under Government influence was the appointment, or recognition, of the luluai as the agent of the Government (Report 1923:40, quoted in Brown 1963:2).

Brown (1972:70) points out that the power of *luluais* and *tultuls,* "depended more upon administration support than upon the authority which they naturally held as big men within their groups." As a result, "tribal leadership changed in a generation from the absence of any fixed authority ('anarchy') to a system giving officials the opportunity to dominate ('satrapy')" (Brown 1963a:3). Brown's (1963a) analysis of the transformation of leadership engendered debate regarding the extent to which the traditional situation throughout the Highlands could be considered "anarchy" (see Salisbury 1964; Strathern 1966; and Brandewie 1971). On the other hand, Brown's characterization of the postcontact period as one of government-backed satraps has seen little criticism. The period of elected councilors that followed the *luluais* can be seen as an attempt to return some control over local leaders to the people.

The original *Native Local Government Councils Ordinance* 1949–1960 authorized councils to maintain peace, order, and good government, but did not provide for specific magisterial duties (M. Strathern 1972a:95). Local government councils are constituted according to the *Local Government Ordinance* 1963, which came into effect in 1965. Under this ordinance, local government councils are charged with the control, management, and administration of the council area. The task of the councilor, therefore, is primarily administrative rather than judicial.

Nevertheless, by advising disputants that cases should be heard by their local councilor, police legitimize the councilor's dispute-handling role. Police in Gumine justify sending cases back to the councilors on four grounds: (a) councilors are best able to deal with matters that concern local custom; (b) in civil matters, settlement is ideally reached through agreement, which is more likely to occur when cases are heard at the local level; (c) in criminal cases, imprisonment may be seriously detrimental to the health of the aged; and (d) officials realize that if they attempted to hear all disputes, the court would be seriously overcrowded.

Considering the low emphasis on third-party intervention in the traditional society, there is little wonder that councilors and *komitis* are considered the only local community members with the "power to straighten the talk," that is, settle disputes.

Moots in Mul

Moots can be heard at any time, though usually they occur early in the morning. Among the Egaku moots are heard on Mondays unless open hostility and the threat of imminent violence demand the councilor's immediate attention. Most frequently, the disputants come to a councilor or *komiti* and ask him to help them settle a dispute. Sometimes the complainant comes to the councilor and the other is summoned.

Normally clan members bring disputes to their own councilor, but this is not required and some councilors and *komitis* who have a particular acumen for handling cases complain of being overburdened.

Although disputants are usually male, women are free to bring complaints to councilors, and they are often involved as principals and witnesses in dispute cases. Casual observers and supporters of the disputants generally sit intermixed unless the issue is volatile, in which case the disputants and their supporters sit a safe distance apart.

The informal atmosphere contrasts with our own legal system. Children play freely during the proceedings, and onlookers wander about, coming and going as they please. Also in contrast to our legal system, everyone in the community understands what goes on at moots because they are frequent public events.

Moots usually begin with the injured party stating the grievance or the councilor reviewing the situation as he understands it. By grievance I mean the *precipitating incident*, the act or event which brought the parties to the moot on this particular occasion. As the talk proceeds, any interested party, male or female, young or old, may comment. Since there is no judge to pronounce comments "irrelevant," people bring up a broad range of related issues. During these discussions past disputes are sometimes recounted, and the "root cause" of the conflict may be revealed. While it is likely that everyone is already aware of long-standing animosities between the disputants, the moot may give the latter the opportunity to air their complaints publicly.

The overt goal of all moots is "settlement" by reducing the victim's anger. Simbu refer to this as "making the belly cold." To make the belly cold, the "victim" (or offended party) must receive compensation. After some discussion, the offended party usually mentions an acceptable price. The offender can then pay up, bargain, or reject the request altogether. The payment is usually in cash, though anything, from chickens to pigs, may be given. Oftentimes onlookers may contribute to the compensation payment. This leads to an acceptable settlement even though the payment is made by others.

Simbu make no distinction between civil and criminal cases. However, as we shall see in chapter 7, compensation payments function differently in categories of cases that we might call civil and criminal.

The role of the councilor is complex. Ideally, he should behave as a neutral third party, though no one really expects him to. He is not selected because he is equally related (structurally intermediate) to both parties, as is the case in the Ndendeuli society discussed by Gulliver (1969b). In fact, the very notion of having one elected councilor for every clan is incompatible with intervention by a third party who is structurally intermediate between the two disputants. He presents himself as a man who understands and follows the new government laws but is, at the same time, cognizant of traditionally appropriate values and behaviors. He should maintain a low profile during the moot, allowing disputants to talk out the grievance, though he must occasionally interject to ask questions that help clarify the issue or to articulate the law of the government as he understands it.

If disputants become intransigent or hostile, the councilor attempts to reconcile them by emphasizing the importance of the social relationship between the disputants. Councilors realize that to truly settle a dispute it must be discussed in full, often involving past issues. Yet, councilors believe that there is a government rule that past grievances should never be brought up during a moot. If the moot does not proceed smoothly to a quick conclusion, councilors may try to cut the talk short by announcing that "it is bad if your mouths become tired and heavy" or "the sun is cooking us and we must all go and work in our gardens."

Although his primary role is one of mediator, a councilor may, at times, suggest a figure that he thinks the offender must pay. Yet he lacks sanctions to enforce such commands.

Gulliver (1977:26) describes the strategies of mediators as lying along a continuum "from virtual passivity to 'chairman', to 'enunciator', to 'prompter', to 'leader', to 'virtual arbitrator'." As he points out, these are not typologies but indices along a continuum. Councilors in Mul make use of all but the last of these strategies, employing them in a decreasing order of frequency. Of course, personalities come into play and some councilors tend to be more or less passive than others. Mediators may also vary their strategies during a particular case.

As a mediator during disputes, the councilor is primarily passive. His presence encourages positive communication and interaction and constrains the parties to observe at least minimal courtesies. At times, the councilor may act in the role of "chairman," keeping order and directing procedure as well as announcing or reiterating points of agreement. The mediator as "enunciator" may go beyond the chairman role by specifying or reciting rules and norms, either traditional or those of the administration. Moreover, mediators often point out that the disputants are "one-blood," or note that "this is not an outside *kot*," meaning that the disputants belong to some inclusive group and should try to cooperate in reaching agreement. In the role of "prompter," the councilor makes suggestions in order to draw the two parties together. Finally, as a "leader" he may attempt to "force" the issue when parties come to an impasse.

If, in the end, the injured party is to receive cash as compensation, the offender and any others making a contribution give the money to the councilor, who then passes this on to the injured party. The injured party may, in certain types of cases, redistribute portions of the payment to others involved in the case.

When the moot is concluded, councilors or other influential people may take the opportunity to discuss or make speeches about community problems that are similar in nature to the preceding case. The problem of people failing to tether their pigs at night was frequently discussed after cases of damage to gardens caused by pigs roaming freely. Increased theft by youngsters was also a common topic of discussion.

Moots, therefore, provide an occasion when the tenets of proper behavior can be publicly disseminated. During a moot over a man who hit his mother, whom he suspected of selling some of his coffee, *Komiti* Kevin made the following pronouncement:

> You people of Simbu—children must look out for their parents and when they are close to death they will thank their children. If you treat them like rubbish, they will think that when you were little they took care of you and cleaned your bowel movements and now you do not treat them well. When they die, they turn their backs on you. If that happens, your fate will be bad. All things you do, like raising children, pigs, and gardens will come out wrong. You must look out for your mother.

Of the sixty-five dispute cases that I recorded, forty-nine (75%) made use of mediation by councilors or *komitis* at some point in the disputing process. I have classified these cases by the nature of the offense as it was presented to the councilor at the opening of the moot.

Most striking is the finding that nearly half (49%) of all disputes aired publicly at moots resulted from damage to property (see table 4-3). Almost invariably, this was a matter of pigs damaging garden crops. This may have important implications for reducing conflict in the Highlands through the improvement of fence construction or pig husbandry practices.

TABLE 4-3   FREQUENCY OF MOOTS CLASSIFIED BY TYPE OF CASE

	N	%
Property damage	24	49
Physical injury	6	12
Theft	5	10
Adulterous behavior	5	10
Land encroachment	3	6
Pig death	2	4
Pig debt	1	2
Threat of injury	1	2
Child custody	1	2
Insult	1	2
Total	49	100

Due to rounding percentages may not add up to 100 percent.

Physical injury, which accounts for 12 percent of all moots, are very different from the stranger assaults that we are used to thinking about. These injuries result from violent responses to a previous grievance. They are in some sense not precipitating incidents but represent the use of coercion. Nevertheless, the primary issue during a moot is often the injury rather than the original offense. For example, a man begins to build a house on the ground belonging to another without securing proper permission first. The owner becomes infuriated and attacks the builder. Everyone knows, including the builder, that he should have gotten prior approval, so he quickly ceases construction. Then he brings a case against his attacker for the injury caused by the attack.

Theft and adulterous behavior, with only 10 percent of the cases each, account for a smaller proportion of the cases heard in moots. Land encroachment, possibly the most serious offense in this densely populated region, accounts for only 6 percent. Thus, among the four central causes of conflict, *there is an inverse relationship between the seriousness of offense and the frequency of its occurrence*.

COURTS AND MOOTS—A BRIEF COMPARISON

T. E. Barnett (1972:61) points out that the Australian administration's insistence upon a highly centralized official court system, run by Australians according to Australian rules without, until recently, any indigenous participation above the level of interpreter, resulted in the development and continuance of a flourishing unofficial court system.

Strathern's (1972a:20; see also 1972b) study of official and unofficial courts in Mt. Hagen concludes that "There is a gap between Hageners' model of the present legal system, and the Administration's (and informed Europeans') model." Where Hageners view the entire system as a hierarchy, administrators view the official legal system and the local moots as qualitatively different. In this rural area of the Simbu Province, five years after Strathern's study, this same dichotomy can be said to exist. Though here it is more one of emphasis.

Magistrates and administrators are, of course, aware of the legal distinction between the official and unofficial dispute processes. Yet, they encourage councilors to settle grievances in the local community when possible. They realize that most grievances that arise in the local community do not reach the official court and that most cases that are heard by the court do not come as "appeals" from the unofficial system.

Local community members are also aware of the qualitative difference between courts and moots. People have occasionally observed police or patrol officers making arrests in the community. They realize this leads to a court process that is quite distinct from local-level dispute processes in terms of both procedure and ideology. Their main concern, however, is with the use of the official court system as an alternative when local processes fail to contain the issue or bring about a settlement. Their focus, therefore, is on the hierarchical nature of the combined system.

These perceptions are manifest in the two ways that cases from local areas reach the official court system. In the first, news reaches the police that a serious breach of the law has occurred. If the police feel that local processes will be unable to contain the conflict, as in instances of serious injury, a party of two to five unarmed police officers is dispatched to the scene. When they reach the area, they inquire into the initial grievance and what has occurred during the conflict. If it seems like a matter that can be resolved locally, they advise the councilor to do so; if the conflict does not seem resolvable, the offender (or offenders) is arrested and brought to the police station along with councilors, witnesses, and others concerned. Upon returning to the police station, charges are filed, and those arrested are put in jail where they are held until able to raise bail or until the case is heard by the magistrate in criminal court.

The second way cases reach the court system is when disputants and councilors bring the case to the police station after attempts to resolve the issue in the local moot have failed. The case is then screened by the officers, who decide how to proceed. It may be referred back to the councilors, sent to the magistrate for informal mediation or hearing in the civil court, or the offender may be arrested and the case placed on the criminal court calendar. The reader will recall that only one of the sixty-five cases (1.5%) recorded in Mul reached the official court.

Administrators and local Simbu have different visions of the local court case load. Administrators are not aware of all the local cases, but see only cases that cannot be resolved locally and have passed through the screening by the police. Local residents, who take their starting point as the community, see all the cases and are aware that the only local cases that go to the courts are those that have been aired at moots but could not be settled.

A second, and I believe important, difference between the official court and the local-level dispute-handling process is the fundamental conception of justice. At the local level the ideal concern is the *settlement* of the grievance—"to make the belly cold" or "to straighten the talk." This can only be achieved, according to Simbu ideology, when the offended party receives a compensation payment that he or she considers satisfactory.

In moots the intended outcome is compensation, while in the criminal courts the intended outcome is punishment of the offender through fine or imprisonment. *During a moot, justice seems to be about things that happen to or for the offended party, whereas in the criminal sector of the official court system justice is about things that happen to perpetrators.* In the court no compensation is offered to the offended party and from his or her point of view the grievance has not been alleviated because compensation has not been received. This understanding of the criminal court is carried over to the civil court and to informal mediation by the magistrate. For this reason disputants and councilors make use of the official court system only when no other alternatives are open to them.

5 / The Social Organization of Conflict Management

The preceding two chapters examined the procedures of dispute handling as though each existed independently. In chapter 3, I described the use of avoidance, coercion, and negotiation as dyadic mechanisms for processing conflict. In chapter 4, I presented two procedures involving third-party intervention—mediation and adjudication. These procedures are the elements that together form a larger dispute-handling system. In those chapters the parts of the system were presented with little regard to their interconnection. While this is important for a clear analysis, it is only a first step in understanding the larger pattern and process of dispute handling.

If one begins at the beginning, that is, with some precipitating incident that brings two individuals into open conflict, one finds that dispute cases often go through a series of stages and make use of a number of mechanisms, or strategies, at different points in the conflict. Indeed, one-third of the cases in my sample make use of more than one type of procedure. The various procedures do not fall into a neat linear hierarchy, but neither are they used in a random fashion. For example, no one ever uses adjudication, the police, or mediation by a magistrate as their first strategy.

The goal in this chapter is to provide an empirically based description of the social organization of dispute handling. I begin with a case and conclude with a flow diagram based on the analysis of sixty-five cases.

In the case that follows, an old man is accused of committing adultery with his nephew's wife. Initial attempts at settlement break down in a most unkinsman-like fashion. As the conflict escalates, the disputants are forced to proceed through several stages. The case is provocative in drawing our attention to a number of issues. We find, for example, that even close kin involved in multiplex social and economic relations may resort to physical violence in response to perceived affronts; we wonder whether this is typical of offenses between kin. The case further leads us to inquire about the ways in which an individual's behavior during a case may alter the substantive issues under dispute as well as how the case is handled. Note the level of authority displayed by councilor and *komiti,* the frequent reference to Gare and Dima as father and son, the reference to this not being an outside dispute, and the outcome—who gets compensation. Did Gare do it?

CASE 3—A CASE OF ADULTERY

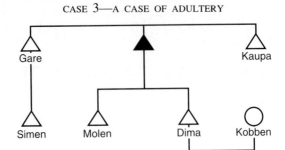

Incident

A dispute erupts when Dima accuses Gare of committing adultery with his wife, Kobben.

Background

Kobben and Dima had been married only three months when this incident took place. When she was young, Kobben had been married to a man from Sina Sina (a neighboring district), but she ran away. Although they were married, Dima had not paid the traditional bride price.

Dima and his father's brother, Gare, are partners in a trade store. Gare is an elderly man of slight build with gray hair and beard. Dima is about thirty to thirty-five years old.

Breach

On the night of April 6, 1977, a Wednesday, Gare and Kobben were at her house while Dima was at the trade store. Gare leaned close to Kobben and whispered in her ear, asking if her husband had given her any money. She replied that he was not in the habit of giving her money. Gare said that if she would pick coffee for him he would give her 90 toea (about U.S. $1.25). When Dima returned, he found the old man close to his wife. (It is unclear exactly what they were doing.) Dima said "You're like my father and hers. Why are you so close to her?" The old man responded that he was just talking to her. "Why are you so angry?" he said.

Angered by Gare's behavior, Dima took his wife to the house of his father's other brother, Kaupa. A short while later Gare arrived at Kaupa's house. Dima directed Gare to sit next to Kobben and show Kaupa what the two of them were doing. Losing his temper, Gare surged forward, attempting to hit Dima. But Dima was younger and stronger than Gare and knocked him down twice. Simen, Gare's son, grabbed Dima and held him back while Gare hit Dima twice in the face. Simen said "That's enough," but Dima became even more angry because he had a bloody nose. Dima's brother, Molen, held Simen and Dima punched him in the eye. The fight ended.

During the fight several injuries occurred: the old man's head was rather bloodied and his middle finger had been quite badly bitten by Dima; Dima had sustained a bloody nose, and Simen came away with a swollen eye.

After the fighting was over, they spoke of being "one-blood" and verbalized ideals that close relatives should not fight with each other. They decided to hold a moot the next day. That night Dima and Kobben stayed at Kaupa's house while the others went home to sleep.

Thursday, April 7, 1977

The next morning all those involved met with Council Sago, *Komiti* Gimbol, and *Komiti* Weway to hold a moot. Gare opened the discussion, saying that he didn't sleep with the woman, "They are lying." Angered by Gare's belligerence, Dima marched off to the police station at Gumine and reported what had occurred. The police dispatched a Land Cruiser to bring the others to the government station.

At Gumine, the disputants went inside the police station, where Dima reported that the old man had slept with his wife. Gare once again said that Dima was lying. One of the officers threatened Gare, saying that if he didn't tell the truth they would put him in jail for two weeks. Afraid of the consequences, the old man confessed (though he still maintains he didn't do it). The police then questioned Kobben, who affirmed that Gare had slept with her (though Simen says she was just covering up for Dima). When asked if he had paid a proper bride price for the woman, Dima responded that he didn't "buy her, she just came." The officer said that since Dima had not paid for the woman, he was entitled to only half compensation. He then told them to leave the police station and let Council Sago set an amount of compensation to be paid by Gare.

Friday April 8, 1977

Early the next morning, the men gathered to hold a moot. The discussion was far more complex than the police officer's order for the councilor to set a price would suggest. The following dialogue permits some insight into the complexity of negotiations. The moot opens with Council Sago recounting what had transpired up to this point.

Dialogue

Council Sago: Before you fought, but now it's over. Dima hit the old man and drew blood. He beat him badly. Then Gare and his son hit Dima. We went to the police station and they looked at Dima and Gare. The police officer said that the two *komiti*s and I should go back to our area and work it out. We all gathered to do that last night, but Gare said he was tired and went inside turning his back on all of us. We all got angry at Gare, but we went to sleep. Now we would like to start the moot this morning. I think

As a big man and a councilor, Council Sago, husband of Gunnabia (shown in a previous photo), acts as a mediator in many dispute cases.

Gare should bring some money and Dima too. Dima should give Gare six kina. Now we've been all over the place talking about this and we're all tired of it. Both of you bring money; we can straighten this, then go about our business.

Dima: It's true. I didn't pay for my wife. First she was married in Sina Sina. She left her child there. But she was sad about leaving her child, so she cut her ear. I didn't buy her she just came. Later I can pay for her. She's my wife, she doesn't roam about. I arranged for her to sleep in Gare's house. My father is dead. Now Gare's like my father and I put my wife in his house. Gare is crazy in the head. I think in the middle of the night he got up and tried to make trouble with my wife.

Council Sago: We've heard this all before. Let's just pay up and straighten things out.

Dima: During the night when I walk about or play dice, I watch my wife inside the house. Gare is always fooling around with her. I've seen it. I'm not talking nothing.

Komiti Weway: Let's stop all this talk before it gets too hot. Both of you go get your money. If you don't bring it, we'll have to talk more later. Stop talking so much. First we must see Gare give money to Dima.

Council Sago: You all want to talk, but I understand all this. I'm the man of the law; I can talk. Suppose I don't talk straight, then you can talk. If we can't straighten it we'll have to go put the old man in jail.

Oury (a young man):   You don't understand the ways of Gare. I live close by and understand. He's another kind of man. If we give money to Dima,

Gare will remain very angry. Dima can give four kina or something to Gare and Gare give some to Dima; it will be okay. If we only give money to Dima, it will not be over.

Council Sago: You didn't fight with someone from another clan, but with a member of your one-blood group. Now I say just bring some money and we'll finish it. But you seem to feel like arguing more. Okay, Dima should bring four kina and give it to Gare.

Oury: Sago, you talk true. They don't have money. Now they can bring coffee and sell it and they'll have money. Then they can give some money to Dima. [One of Gare's children hands Oury ten kina and another son contributes six kina more. Oury passes the sixteen kina to Council Sago. A long silent period follows.]

Oury: I've got sixteen kina for Dima. Do you see it?

Dima: It's not my place to look at the money. I'm not the Councilor.

Gare: I'm an old man, I'm not a young man after your wife. I will give you money; you can take it. If you want more I don't have it. I'll go to jail. If I die, my children can have my place. She's your wife, but you didn't buy her. I didn't make trouble with her. If I did, I would tell you.

Oury: All right, we want to straighten this. Stop all the talk. You are an old man.

Molden: Half the moot is over, we must talk softly. The councilor and *komiti* can straighten it. It will be over. If we talk strongly, the *komiti*s and councilors will not be able to straighten it. Gare must bring twenty kina and give it to Dima. Then it will be over.

Dima: Before, I gave Gare 12 kina when he needed it during another moot. So, if Gare gives me twenty kina, it is twelve kina to pay me back and only eight for this moot.

Gare: Dima and I own a trade store together. I've been involved in many moots lately. I've no more money in the store. Dima has seen it. I don't hide any money. Now I'll sell a little coffee and then I can give you the money.

Dima: Very true. You are an old man. All the others have died and you're still alive. If you go into jail you'll die and I'll be very sad. Council Sago and *Komiti* Weway are here and they can straighten it. It would not be good to go to the police station and put you in jail. It would be bad if you die.

Council Sago: True, young men can go to jail. But very old men can't. They die and then we're all very sad. If you go to Gumine you may have to pay one hundred kina and go to jail too. We'll settle this here.

Dima: If young men get put in jail, we know how to work. We get up and work and it's all right. We work strong. You old men can't go to jail.

Many men begin to shout: This talk is going on too long. We're tired of it.

Oury: Each man is talking too much. We're all one-blood. Cut the talk and then we can go about our business.

Council Sago: Gare and his children must bring some money so we can finish this moot.

Komiti Weway: This is not a moot between outsiders, just us. Bring a little money and let's finish.

Dima: That's true. He can give me a little money and it's over. I'm tired of this.

Kai: Okay, sixteen kina are here, let's find four kina more and give Dima twenty kina. Let's stop all this long talking, we're losing too much time. Find four kina more and it's finished.

Molden: They've brought sixteen kina. Can you people from outside help him with four kina more?

Kai: You are all one-blood. Gare is like a father to all of you. We don't often help Gare with money. Now he has fought with his "child"; we must all hurry up and give him some money so he can give it to Dima.

Komiti Weway: That's right. Just find some money. Yesterday there was a moot and we spent all our money. If we had some money we would help him, but we really don't. I'm not lying. We really don't have money.

Gare: Many big-men have come and weren't able to hit me. Now Dima comes, bites my hand, and draws blood. I am very angry about this. I'm an old man. If you hit me a little, that's okay, but you hit me too much and I'm sick now.

Kai: Yesterday you went to the police station. That's enough. All the men in Gumine looked at us and asked why an old man with white hair was beat up by his "son."

Gare: I'm an old man. I don't have too much money. I had some, but my pig went in a garden and I had to give all my money away. I have none left. I've got a little and he can have it. If he wants to put me in jail, that's up to him. You are all good men. I don't want you to have to talk too much and your mouths begin to hurt.

Molden: Dima knows that his father is dead and Gare is like his father. He thinks he can put his wife in Gare's house and he will look out for her. If an outside man comes, Gare must look out for her. Now Gare has played around with her and that is no good. Now this comes up and Dima is very cross.

Gare: I give money, and you don't want to take it. Do you want a pig to make this talk end? Before, you gave me a pig. I have it. Do you want it back? All right, I have fed it. If you want it back, you must pay me something.

Simen: Never mind. You are an old man; stop talking and let's go work in our gardens.

Molden: If you want the pig, you must give Gare thirty kina.

Simen: Molden talks true. If Dima wants the pig, he must give Gare thirty kina. That's what I think, too.

Gare: I want to give you money, you don't want it. I want to give you a pig, you don't want it. What do you want? I'm a very old man and don't have much. You think I'm a rubbish man, but I'm no rubbish man. My name is Gare! All know me well.

Simen: Forget it, just go bring some money.

Council Sago: Dima, do you want your pig back or do you want money?

Don't put your nose down; you must look straight and talk straight so we can finish. I'm tired of all this talk. You didn't fight with sticks or bow and arrow. Just with your hands and drew blood. Dima and Gare both hit each other. So it's really even.

Dima: This pig. I gave it to Gare. We can't talk about two different moots now. Later, when Gare has coffee money, he can give me the fourteen kina and the pig will be his altogether. Now we're talking about my wife and that's all.

Komiti Weway: Let's stop talking. Dima, will you take twenty kina? It's up to you. Think about it. If you like, we must give it to you. This pig, take it to market, sell it and split the money some way. Is that okay? If that's not all right, Gare must give Dima some money.

Molden: Dima thinks that Gare played with his wife. He wants money from Gare, not from all the other men. Then it will be over.

Gare: I'm not a troublemaker. I'm an old man. I didn't play with Dima's wife. I'm not lying under the eye of the council.

Komiti Weway: You said all that before. Never mind. Let's just handle it now. You are old. Are you deaf? We've heard it before.

Gare: I don't have any money. My children don't have any money. If they did, they would help me.

Molden: We've heard Gare say he doesn't have any money. We are all one-blood; we must find some money and help Gare. Then we can see how much we get and see if Dima wants it.

Council Sago: We went to the police station and they said Gare must find money and give it to Dima. Dima must find a bit and give it to Gare. The police said that and you all heard it.

Molden: I didn't go to the police station. So that's what they said. Okay, so now let's straighten it like that.

Komiti Weway: Okay, now you of Gare's line must find thirty kina and give it to Dima. I'd like to give some, but I spent it all on a moot yesterday.

Council Sago and Komiti Weway talk at once: All of Gare's people must give one or two kina so Gare can give it to Dima.

Gare: You are all good men. You help me. Later, I'll pay back all the money. Now I don't have money.

Kai: Dima gave twelve kina to Gare before. Now at this moot Gare should give twenty kina to Dima. The two twelve-kina's balance out and eight kina are left. That's up to *Komiti* and council.

Molden: All right, first Dima helped you [Gare] with six kina. Now he can give you six kina because he hit you and drew blood. Now give him twenty kina, but it's really only eight kina.

Gare: Dima doesn't want to pay for hitting me. He's only thinking of receiving pay for his wife. All right, give him the money. I think that he doesn't want to pay for my blood. He can give me a little and I'll be somewhat happy.

Council Sago: Okay, you give him money and he'll give you a bit; then you must shake hands.

Gare: I don't usually fight with Dima. This is the first time. I didn't take his blood, he just hit me in the eye and I fell down. I got up and went to hit him, but he opened his mouth and bit my hand. Now my finger is injured quite a bit. So I called Simen. Simen hit Dima hard. Dima hit Simen hard. They fought.

Molden: You fought like that. You told it at police station and at the moot here. I'm tired of hearing it. I don't want to be cross with everyone. I walk softly. Suppose you give some money to Dima and Dima gives some to you. Do you want compensation from Dima? Tell us what you want. Now you don't have money and we don't either. Okay, sixteen kina have already been collected and Council Sago is holding it. Now find two or four kina more. If we get twenty kina, we can give it to Dima.

Gare: I'm an old man and don't have money.

Komiti Weway: One woman wants to give you two kina. I heard it. Let's ask her. [A young boy asks the woman. She hands him the money and he brings it to Council Sago.] So now we have eighteen kina. [Many men talk in rapid succession and at the same time.]

Komiti Weway: We've been talking. Now this woman gives two kina and the boy gives two kina. That's twenty kina altogether. Let's give it to Dima now.

Molden: We can give this twenty kina to Dima, and he can give four kina to Gare now. [Turning to Gare, he asks:] Do you want four kina or not?

Gare (angrily):   I don't want it! You all split it up.

Oury: That's the custom of the old men.

The men agree that they can now give Dima the twenty kina. The money is placed on the ground and straightened into neat piles. Council Sago hands sixteen kina to Dima and four kina to Gare.

THE STRUCTURE OF OPPORTUNITY

As this case shows, disputants may make use of a number of alternative procedures in their attempt to manage or resolve a conflict. Coercion, mediation, and appeal to the police were all part of the process used in this particular example.

The organization of dispute institutions can be derived by diagraming each of the sixty-five observed cases and compiling these into a single flow chart. In this way, we can generate an empirically based model of the organizational structure of conflict management processes.

All disputes begin with a precipitating incident, or at least the perception of such an incident. It is certainly true that disputes may derive from conflicts of interest and conflicts of values, but these conflicts do not become disputes in the absence of an incident—some behavior on the part of an individual we may call the offender (or his agent). The precipitating incident in the previous case was Gare's behavior toward Kobben, as it was perceived by Dima.

The second element in the social construction of a dispute is the awareness of the behavior (action or event) and the perception of the behavior as offensive. Many behaviors are intrinsically offensive, while others are only offensive in a particular social context. When Dima observed Gare whispering closely in his wife's ear, he took offense and accused Gare of adulterous behavior. This accusation may have arisen out of earlier suspicions based on his own observations or reports of others.

Once an individual becomes aware of some behavior and defines it as offensive, she or he enters into what I call a *grievance situation*. A grievance is a "cause of uneasiness or distress felt to afford rightful reason for reproach, complaint, or resistance" (Webster's Third New International Dictionary, unabridged, 1970). The grievance situation includes the grievance itself as well as all the socially relevant variables (or factors) that affect decisions about how next to respond.

In the case at hand, Dima's response was first to hold a private (in the sense that it was within the extended family) discussion with Gare. During the discussion, interaction degenerated into argument and insult, resulting in violence. The injuries sustained during the scuffle precipitated a new grievance. Once it became clear that the parties would not be able to handle the case through nonviolent negotiations, a moot was arranged the next day. But even mediation was unsuccessful, and Dima decided to take his case to the police station. The police acted as gatekeepers, using their own form of pressure to keep Dima from insisting that the case be heard in the official court. At the officers' insistence, the dispute was rerouted back to the councilor for a second try at mediation.

This series of events resulted from the choices of individuals. The various options open to them were not used in a random fashion. Initial choices were guided by social and situational factors. Once the initial choice was made, new alternatives opened and other options closed. The case proceeded through various stages and then looped back, returning to one of the earlier procedures.

Each of the sixty-five observed cases was analyzed in this fashion. When the data are aggregated, they provide an empirical description of observed events and, at the same time, describe the options for pursuing a grievance. The result is a model of the social organization of conflict management institutions and the flow of the cases through the system (see figure 5-1). The flow chart identifies events, like going to the police, the points at which decisions are made by the disputing parties, and the alternatives open to them at each point in the process. I refer to the lines connecting the boxes as action paths. At each point disputants must weigh all the factors and make choices as to which path to follow in pursuit of the grievance. At any point the offended party has the option of dropping the issue if he or she feels the gains will not override the costs of pursuing the matter any further.

Frequencies have been provided along the action paths. All action paths are unidirectional. It is possible for disputants to make a series of choices leading the case back to a forum through which it had previously passed. A person cannot, however, erase his or her actions from the minds of others. The grievance situation in the second instance is, therefore, not the same as it was in the first.

Let us take a closer look at the pattern. The initial actions in the sixty-five cases are distributed across five options. The least frequent response involved coercion through appeal to the supernatural. In one case, described earlier, Council Sago threatened the use of sorcery if the stolen pandanus fruit were not returned. When

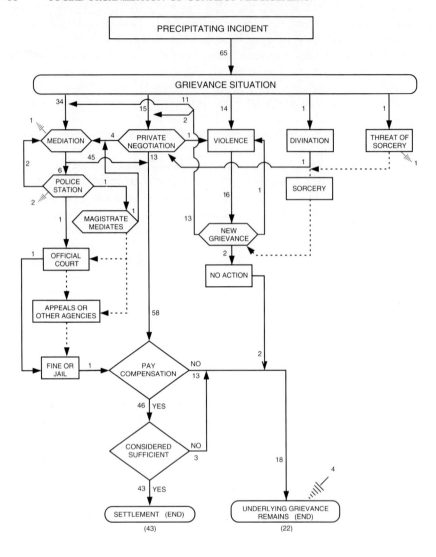
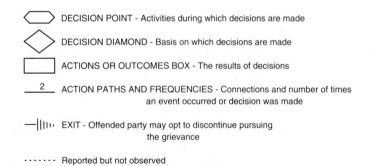

Figure 5-1 Options for Pursuing a Grievance

nothing came of the threats, Sago simply dropped the issue. In a second case, the victim used divination and made a private visit to negotiate a settlement involving a compensation payment. The accused paid no compensation and the underlying grievance remained.

In fourteen cases, the victim's initial response to the grievance was violent retaliation. In addition, violence erupted after negotiations in one case. Thus, in fifteen cases, violence precipitated a new grievance (in one of these the further response was a return act of violence, but there were still only fifteen cases in total). In two cases, disputants took no further action and the underlying grievance remained, while in thirteen cases the dispute proceeded to other forums. Following their violent confrontations, disputants sat down privately to negotiate an agreement in two cases, while in eleven cases a third party acted as mediator.

In fifteen cases, the disputants' first course of action was private negotiations, and three additional cases were negotiated following other actions. Mediation at a public moot followed negotiation in four cases.

Disputants used third-party mediation in a public setting more frequently than any other procedure. Mediation was the first choice in thirty-four cases; mediation followed violence in eleven cases and negotiation in four cases. A total of forty-nine cases, at some point, were publicly aired at a moot.

Disputants brought six cases to the police station. In no instance did disputants bring a case to the police station without first trying to resolve the conflict at a local moot. *In this sense, the structural relationship between the moot and the police is hierarchical, while the relationship between the moot (mediation) and negotiation or coercion is not.*

The police act as gatekeepers, directing traffic between the local, unofficial court system and the official court system. In two cases, described earlier in this chapter, the disputants were convinced by the police that their councilor should attempt to mediate the cases once again. In two other cases the disputants opted out and decided not to pursue matters any further.

Two cases actually got past the police. One of these was referred to the magistrate, who agreed to mediate informally in his office. The magistrate discussed the matter and then urged the disputants to use local mediation, which they did.

Of the sixty-five dispute cases, only one proceeded past the police and into the official court system.

TABLE 5-1   DISPUTE OUTCOMES

	N	%
Apparent settlement	43	66
Grievance remains		
Dispute processed	18	28
Issue dropped	4	6
Total	65	100

While process has been the primary focus of this chapter, something does need to be said about the outcomes of these cases. A total of fifty-eight cases reached the "pay compensation decision diamond." In forty-six of these cases compensation was paid and in thirteen it was not. In forty-three of the forty-six cases, the compensation received by the offended party seemed to have been sufficient to bring about a "settlement" of the issue at hand. In three cases, the offended party accepted the compensation but made it clear that the amount was not considered sufficient and that the underlying grievance remained. Table 5-1 summarizes the outcomes of the sixty-five cases.

Of the sixty-five cases, forty-three were settled in the sense that the dispute was brought to a conclusion and the parties felt the outcome to be acceptable. Eighteen cases were processed through the system, but, because compensation was not paid or because it was considered insufficient, it is likely that the grievance remained. Finally, in four cases the offended party opted out and the case was not processed to its conclusion and it is likely that the grievance remained.

In sum, the flow diagram is important for two reasons. First, it provides a model of a conflict management system, revealing that there are a number of options for pursuing a grievance and showing how the various parts of the system are interrelated. Second, it provides an empirical and quantitative picture of the movement of cases through the system.

I find that the case load in one part of the system (such as mediation) is dynamically related to occurrences in other parts of the system (such as negotiation). The diagram does not provide, even at the macro level, any *explanation* of the distribution of cases. Why do some cases lead first to violence while others to mediation? What factors guide the decisions and strategies of conflict behavior? To address these questions, I turn, in the next chapter, to the microsociological level. Rather than exemplifying options and institutions, the focus is on a more fine-grained analysis of process.

6 / The Disputing Process

Violence, payback killing, sorcery, and cannibalism are often thought to characterize conflict in the New Guinea Highlands (Berndt 1962, 1965; Koch 1970, 1974; Hayano 1973; Lindenbaum 1971). But, in fact, if one examines frequency rather than flamboyance, a more mundane picture emerges. The initial action in 52 percent of the observed cases is mediation, and an additional 23 percent use negotiation in their first attempt at settlement.

Two factors begin to account for this distribution. First, over half of the cases involve pigs damaging gardens. Such cases, generally speaking, can be settled by paying compensation for the damaged food. Second, the frequency of conflict is inversely related to structural distance: 41 percent of the cases are between members of the same one-blood group and an additional 16 percent are between members of the same subclan. Overall, 78 percent of the conflicts are between members of the same clan. The trend toward conflict with members of one's own group is attributed to the tendency toward localization of land holdings and residence described in chapter 2. It is far more likely that neighbors will come into conflict than individuals who live far apart.

As we examine particular categories of grievance, we find that ideals of appropriate behavior cannot explain, in any simple way, who comes into conflict with whom and how certain people will interact in times of conflict. Ideally, for example, individuals should not encroach upon the land of their "brothers," though the land of a member of a different tribe is fair game. Similarly, the community exerts more pressure for the peaceful resolution of conflicts within the group than between members of different groups. Nevertheless, 75 percent of the land encroachment cases are between members of the same one-blood group, and violence is the first response of the offended party in three-quarters of the land cases, despite close kinship relations.

Table 6-1 classifies the sixty-five disputes according to the nature of the grievance as disputants described it.

The case materials in this chapter are organized according to the main categories of grievance. During the discussion of each category, I will point out that certain types of disputes occur more frequently between persons who are closely related than would be expected by chance alone. The closeness of a relationship refers to the *structural distance* between disputants.

As I have shown in chapter 2, individuals think and interact in terms of group affiliations rather than genealogical connections. The Simbu, for example, describe how a person should act toward another member of an individual's own one-blood group, whereas Americans would describe how one should act toward an uncle. It is

TABLE 6-1   FREQUENCY OF CASES CLASSIFIED BY TYPE OF GRIEVANCE

Type of Grievance	N	%
Property damage by animals	34	52.3
Theft	8	12.3
Adulterous behavior	5	7.7
Land encroachment	4	6.2
Domestic disputes*	4	6.2
Insult	4	6.2
Disputes over children	2	3.1
Disputes over cards	1	1.5
Pig killed by car	1	1.5
Pig debt	1	1.5
Child custody	1	1.5
Total	65	100.0

*Includes disputes between husband and wife and between co-wives.

TABLE 6-2   FREQUENCY OF DISPUTES CLASSIFIED BY STRUCTURAL DISTANCE

Structural Distance	N	%
Same subclan section	30	41.0
Same subclan/different sections	12	16.4
Same clan/different subclans	15	20.5
Same tribe/different clans	11	15.1
Different tribes	5	6.8
Total	73	100.0

Due to rounding percentages may not add up to 100 percent.

possible, therefore, to prioritize the importance of relationships according to structural distance. Members of the same subclan section (one-blood group) are closer than individuals who are members of the same subclan but different sections; members of the same subclan are closer than members of the same clan, and so on.

Table 6-2 shows the distribution of disputes by structural distance. Since a single case sometimes included more than two disputants, such as when more than one pig goes into a garden, there are a total of seventy-three relationships, even though there were only sixty-five cases.

PROPERTY DAMAGE BY ANIMALS

Over one-half (34 out of 65, or 52.3 percent) of all cases involved the destruction of property by animals. All but two of these involved pigs going into gardens, sometimes by breaking a fence, and eating copious quantities of sweet potatoes, taro, yams, or sugar cane.

TABLE 6-3   PROPERTY DAMAGE BY ANIMALS CLASSIFIED BY STRUCTURAL DISTANCE

Structural Distance	N	%
Same subclan section	20	40.8
Same subclan/different sections	8	16.3
Same clan/different subclans	14	28.3
Same tribe/different clans	7	14.3
Different tribes	0	0
Total	49	100.0

Due to rounding percentages may not add up to 100 percent.

On some occasions, pigs belonging to more than one owner went into a garden. When this occurred, the garden owner brought all the pig owners together (if possible) and the case was handled as if only one pig had caused all the damage. For this reason, I classified each such case as a single case in the present analysis. The thirty-two cases included forty-seven people whose pigs had damaged gardens. Adding the two "nonpig" cases makes a total of forty-nine "offenders" in cases of property damage by animals.

Table 6-3 classifies these thirty-four cases according to the structural distance between the disputants. In twenty instances (41%), the animals damaged the property of a person who was in the same subclan section as their owner. This is attributed to the tendency toward localization of the members of the subclan section rather than to any knowledge on the pig's part. In fact, people readily point out that "pigs have no sense" but merely smell the food and go into the garden. They also point out that once a pig goes into a garden, it is likely to remember the place and return to it again.

Because pigs have no sense, people do not take affront when a pig damages their crops. Pig owners are, however, considered responsible for the actions of their pigs and should do their utmost to prevent damages to the gardens of others.

A series of three short cases between the same disputants highlights this point. In each of these cases, the owners of the pig are Gui and his wife, An. The owners of the garden are Koma Sago and his wife, Sine. Both men are members of the Naraku clan, Kune subclan, and Dabile subclan section.

CASE 4—THE CASE OF THE HUNGRY HOG

On May 7, 1977, a pig belonging to Gui Dema Galima went into the bush garden of Koma Sago. Koma's wife, Sine, saw the pig in the garden and went to tell her husband. Together they went to see Gui privately. At first Koma asked for a K 10.00 compensation payment for the damaged crops, but when Gui said that he did not have that much money, Koma accepted K 4.00, which he handed directly to Sine.

As far as all parties were concerned, the case was settled. Two weeks later, however, the same pig again went into the same garden. And again the disputants negotiated privately.

CASE 5—THE HUNGRY HOG RETURNS

On May 19, 1977, Gui's pig again went into Koma's garden. As before, Koma, Gui, and their two wives, An and Sine, discussed the matter privately. The disputants spoke of the recent Gumine Local Government Council suggestion that the appropriate rate of compensation for garden damage by pigs is K 10.00. They also expressed their relations as "brothers" and arrived at a price of K 6.00. Gui paid Koma, who passed the compensation money to his wife. The case had been brought to an amicable conclusion.

During this case, as in the one previously, all was amicable and the case was considered settled by the payment of compensation arrived at by mutual agreement. However, fourteen days later Gui's pig went into Koma's garden for the third time. This time Koma became irate and appeared ready to fight with Gui. Sine returned the K 6.00 that she had received in the previous case and complained that the garden was now ruined altogether and a large compensation payment would be required. A moot was convened at the Mul ceremonial ground with Council Sago acting as mediator. The moot was opened by the offended party, Koma.

CASE 6—FURTHER ADVENTURES OF THE HUNGRY HOG

Dialogue

Koma: I am telling the truth. There is nothing left in the garden. The pig turned up all the ground and ate everything. Now I will let the grass come up and then plant a new garden.

Council Sago: Gui, you understand. If your pig goes into a garden and eats a little only once, then you can just fix the fence. But now your pig is too strong and finished off the whole garden. You must give a large compensation payment. That is the law. Now there is no garden left, so Koma thinks there is no reason you must rebuild the fence. Just give him a payment.

   The law says that if your pig goes into a garden and you fix the fence quickly, the compensation payment required will be small. That is what the law book says. Now your pig went inside the garden a third time and there is no use in rebuilding the fence. You must give a payment to Koma.

   When Koma planted the garden, I helped bring wood for the fence. He planted cabbage, beans, onions, *pit pit,* sweet potatoes, taro, and greens, and they were all coming up well. This is good ground. It is close to the bush. I saw, with my own eyes, that the sweet potatoes were large good ones.

Koma: I have already harvested some of the greens and cabbage and given it out. The sweet potatoes were almost ready and I was going to give them out to people, but now the pig has eaten them and so I cannot give any to you.

It is a long way to this garden. You must travel over two mountains to get there. I would like to give K 4.00 to Council Sago so he can go over there and look at the garden. You [all] think I am fooling so I can give you [Council Sago] K 2.00 [sic] so you can go to see the garden and know that I am not lying.

Sine: That is right! We can give you K 4.00 so you can go look at the garden.

Council Sago: Before, you came and reported this and said we should go look at the garden. Now I hear you say it again. Before, you brought the leaves and vines from the damaged plants to show me and to Council Maima [Malaku clan] as well.

Gui has some money. If you want it, let us finish this quickly so we can bring your father to the aid post.

[Koma's father, old Sago, is sick. A stretcher has been constructed and they were about to bring him to the aid post at Gumine when this moot began.]

[Gui leans over to Council Sago and tells him that he has brought K 10.00 to give to Koma.]

Council Sago: Gui has K 10.00. Do you want it or is it not enough money?

Sine: You talk of K 10.00 but Old Sago [Koma's father] was sick and so we spent it in one day on blankets and things. K 10.00 is not much. I do not want K 10.00.

Council Sago: All right, if you do not want the K 10.00, let us bring the old man to the aid post.

[Gui leans over to Council Sago and tells him that he has K 8.00 more which he can give to Koma.]

Council Sago: Gui says he will give K 8.00 more. That is K 18.00. Is that enough?

Sine: You are the councilor. You must go look at the garden first. I worked hard to plant this garden on good ground close to the bush. Now it is all ruined.

Council Sago: I asked Gui if the garden was ruined. He said he had seen it and that it was true that it was totally ruined.

Yobai Onus: I have seen the garden and can say that it was a really good one with large sweet potatoes.

Sine: One time a small animal came into the garden but it only ate a little, by the edge. Now this pig has come into the garden and eaten everything.

Council Sago: Tomorrow we will go look at the garden.

[On Saturday, I went with Council Sago, Koma, and Gui to look at the garden. All agreed that the pig had ruined the garden. Gui agreed to kill a pig and give it to Koma at a moot the next day. However, on Sunday Gui came to the moot at the Mul ceremonial ground with cash rather than the promised pig.]

Council Sago: Yesterday I went and looked at the garden. I went to Gui's house and he said that he would like to give Koma a small pig. I thought that, since they are members of the same one-blood group, Gui should not give Koma a pig because people may think it is too much pay and another argument may come up later. But, Gui said he wanted to give Koma a small pig. I went home thinking that it would be better if Gui killed the pig and sold it in the market. Then he could give Koma the proper payment and keep the rest for himself.

If this happened during the time of our grandparents, we could kill the pig and give it to the garden owner. But that is not the way we do it now.

On Friday, Gui brought K 18.00 but Koma did not want it. Now he has brought K 6.00 more. That is K 24.00 altogether. This is not up to me. It is up to the owner of the garden. Do you want the K 24.00 or not? If you do not want it, you must speak up quickly because it is starting to rain.

Koma: Before, I did not want the K 18.00. I do not want to talk angrily again. Gui is not from outside. He is my one-blood. It is not up to me, but up to my wife. If she wants the K 24.00, then we will take it.

Sine: The pig went inside the garden. The garden is far away so Koma could not go to fix the fence quickly. The food is all eaten. It is not good for us to talk a long time and become angry. Gui brought K 24.00 and he can give it to me.

Council Sago: I saw the garden and there was really no good fence, so it was easy for the pig to go inside. The fence is your [Koma's] responsibility, but if you want you can come and take the money.

Sine: It is our garden, true. But we gave parts to four other women, and their husbands did not come and make the fence. I do not want to keep talking because Gui will get tired of us.

Council Sago: I thought, last night, that if Gui gave Koma a pig, he [Gui] would be angry and not tie up his other pigs and they would continue to ruin gardens. Now if you pay the money, you can all go and rebuild the fence and plant a new garden again.

Gui: If a pig of ours goes into the garden of an outsider, we can talk a long time [become hostile]. But we are "brothers" and my pig ruined your garden. My big pigs did not go in the garden, just a few small ones. If the big ones had gone in, we could kill them. The small pigs were out foraging for insects, and when they came back they could walk right into the garden because there was no fence.

Now I have given you the money and you can help me and together we will go put a fence around the garden. I thought of bringing my pig, but it is not fat and I was ashamed for people to see it. If we work together, we can rebuild the fence.

I remember that Sine gave me food from her garden so I want to help rebuild the fence.

[Gui gives the money to Council Sago, who hands it to Koma, who, in turn, divides K 9.00 among the four women who had gardens on his plot of land and then gives the rest to his wife, Sine.]

By examining this series of three cases, we are able to observe how grievances affect and redefine social relations between the individual disputants. It is clear that in the first two cases the disputants, realizing that "pigs have no sense," emphasized their close relationship as members of the same one-blood group. After the third incident, however, Koma was disgruntled because Gui had not taken adequate precautions by restraining his pigs during the night. In a sense this was an affront because Gui was not adequately looking out for the property of his "brother."

Notice that K 24.00, which was accepted, less the K 4.00, which they said they would give to Council Sago, is only K 2.00 more than the K 18.00 offered by Gui during the first session of the moot. It is obvious that having all parties trek to the bush garden was intended for more than reaffirming the "facts," which everyone had previously conceded. Though a few vines of the damaged crop are usually brought to the moot as "evidence," this is the only case in which disputants actually went to a garden to assess the damage. Moreover, Gui's offer to give Koma a pig may been seen as an attempt to restore his own prestige and to indicate to Koma his strong desire to restore the amicable relations which had existed between them. To give a piglet, valued at K 20.00, is a symbolic gesture that goes beyond the giving of an equivalent in cash.

THEFT

I recorded eight disputes over theft (12.3% of all cases) during the field period. Although theft is nothing new in Simbu, only three of the eight cases involved the theft of traditional items: garden produce (2 cases) and a pig (1 case). The five remaining cases involved nontraditional items; in two of the eight cases, the offenders were young boys. In two cases, which made use of the supernatural, the victim did not accuse any particular individual. Table 6-4 describes the remaining six cases.

TABLE 6-4   CASES OF THEFT CLASSIFIED BY STRUCTURAL DISTANCE

Structural Distance	N	%
Same subclan section	2	33.3
Same subclan/different section	1	16.7
Same clan/different subclan	0	0.0
Same tribe/different clan	1	16.7
Different tribe	2	33.3
Total	6	100.0

Unlike property damage cases, these six show no association between the frequency of theft and the structural distance between disputants (see table 6-4).

CASE 7—THE CASE OF THE WAYLAID PIG

Boi had left two of his pigs with a matrilateral kinsman at a place called Dowa. The two pigs left Dowa together. One arrived home, but the other did not. Four months later, Boi's wife found the second pig at Deri. She asked who the pig belonged to and was told that it was Alua's. She then asked Alua where he had purchased it. Alua replied that the pig had been lost and that he took it in and cared for it. With little said, she returned home and informed her husband of what she had learned. Boi returned to Deri with Council Kora (Egaku clan) and a moot was convened.

During the moot Boi said that the two pigs were returning home, that one had arrived but Alua had stolen the other. The argument became heated.

Council Kora said that since Alua had not killed the pig he must now return it to its rightful owner. He added, furthermore, that since Alua had kept the pig for four months without informing its owner, he must pay compensation as well. Alua argued that he had no money but Council Kora suggested that he find some so that the moot could be concluded quickly.

Alua was able to collect K 10.00, which he handed to Council Kora. Not to be completely outdone, Alua then demanded payment for feeding Boi's pig for four months. Council Kora responded that Boi should not have to pay compensation because Alua stole the pig rather than Boi asking him to look after it for him. Alua conceded that, though he wanted pay, he "hears the words of the Councilor and it is all right."

In this case, Boi not only obtained the return of his pig and was spared having to feed it for four months, but he also received K 10.00 compensation. Although Alua waylaid the pig on its way home, he did not come, under the cover of darkness, to steal the pig away from Egaku territory. Indeed, Alua may not, in fact, have been aware of the pig's rightful owner. While these facts may have mitigated in his favor, compensation was still a prerequisite to the conclusion of the dispute.

ADULTEROUS BEHAVIOR

The definition of adultery as "voluntary sexual intercourse between a married man and someone other than his wife or between a married woman and someone other than her husband" (Webster's Third New International Dictionary, unabridged, 1970) is certainly not acceptable for cross-cultural purposes.

Marriage in Simbu is polygynous—men are permitted more than one wife. After marriage, men may continue to participate in courting activities. A sexual relationship between a married man and an unmarried woman is not an adulterous relationship. A sexual relationship between a married woman and either a married or

TABLE 6-5   ADULTEROUS BEHAVIOR CLASSIFIED BY STRUCTURAL DISTANCE

Structural Distance	N	%
Same subclan section	4	80
Same subclan/different section	1	20
Same clan/different subclan	0	0
Same tribe/different clan	0	0
Different tribe	0	0
Total	5	100

unmarried man is adulterous and is not condoned. The marital status of the woman, therefore, determines whether a sexual relationship is, or is not, considered adulterous behavior in Mul. We may conclude that Simbu culture defines adulterous behavior as sexually oriented advances or sexual intercourse between a man and a married woman other than his wife. I recorded five cases (7.7% of all cases) of adulterous behavior.

In all cases, the man (rather than the married woman) was considered the offender and the husband was the complainant. In two cases, however, where the husband was not in the local area, the woman, herself, acted as a complainant. A wife does not, typically, become a complainant if her husband commits adultery.

Table 6-5 shows that cases of adulterous behavior are far more likely to occur between persons who are structurally close, particularly members of the same subclan section. I attribute this to the volatile nature of this type of grievance. Adulterous advances toward a woman are considered an affront to the prestige of the husband as well as his social group.

Within the one-blood group, adulterous advances toward the wife of a "brother" are serious offenses and should not be condoned by other members of the group. However, if it occurs, parties can be reconciled by a compensatory payment, which, in effect, is an indication that the offender wishes to make amends and serves to restore the prestige of the husband. Advances toward married women of other groups are not offensive to the man's own group and, therefore, as structural distance increases so does the permissibility of such actions vis à vis the offender's own social group. Obviously, however, the woman's husband and her group may be offended.

As the notion of segmentary opposition suggests, the greater the social distance the greater the likelihood the act will be viewed as an offense against the group and, concomitantly, the greater the irreconcilability of the parties and the likelihood of violent hostility. Certainly, at this point, the history of past relations between the opposing groups plays an important role.

In short, disputes of this nature between persons who are structurally close can be settled, while such a dispute between structurally distant parties may lead to fighting or, minimally, require a large compensation payment.

Each of the following three cases reveals interesting turns of events in the process of dispute handling.

CASE 8—THE INTRANSIGENT ADMIRER

Mosmina Gelua (Egaku clan, Maima Gaulin subclan, Kobulamable section) had gone to Lae [a city on the coast of Papua New Guinea] seeking wage labor while his wife, Kabia, remained at home. On Friday night, March 11, 1977, Nera [also of the Kobulamable section] came to Kabia's house, bringing five pieces of firewood. He called to Kabia and offered her the firewood, saying he would like to come inside. Kabia replied that he could not come inside and that the house belonged to one of his "brothers." But Nera was insistent. At last, Kabia relented and told him to come inside and sit down. Nera entered and sat on Kabia's bed. After a few minutes, Kabia went outside, shut the door to her house, and locked Nera inside. She then called for all the people to come look, saying that she was a married woman and all the people should come see the man she had locked in her house.

People came and asked Nera why he, a married man, had gone into a married woman's house. He hid his face and explained that he was just bringing firewood.

Monday morning, a moot was convened by Council Kora of the Egaku clan. Discussion centered around the payment of compensation, but Nera was intransigent. At last, Council Kora advised Nera that he had broken the law by going into Kabia's house and that he *must* pay compensation to her. Nera responded that he had nothing to give.

Since the case could not be settled locally, all parties walked to the police station at Gumine. The police put Nera in jail and advised Council Kora and Kabia to return on Wednesday. The case was not heard until the following Monday, as there was, at this time, no official magistrate in Gumine and the District Officer was burdened with holding court as well as his normal duties.

On the day of the court hearing, Council Kora and Kabia came to Gumine, but, as Nera pleaded guilty, their testimony was not needed. As a result, Kabia never entered the courtroom and, in fact, because of the large number of people who had gathered outside the courthouse, could not get close enough to observe the proceedings.

Nera was convicted and fined K 14.00. In default of payment he was sentenced to one month in jail.

During the moot, Council Kora's behavior shifted from that of the typical passive mediator to that of an arbitrator who has the authority to pronounce a decision. When his decision was not followed, the councilor brought the case to the police, who, in effect, backed his decision. During the court proceedings, Nera pleaded guilty and did not claim that he had been merely bringing firewood. Kabia received no compensation and as a result felt only partially satisfied by the outcome of the case. Several informants with whom I later discussed the case agreed that had the intruder been from another clan, fighting might have erupted.

CASE 9—ADDING INSULT TO ADULTERY

Case 9 concerns a man, Kaupa, (Naraku clan, Kumai subclan, Sagkane subclan section) who entered the house of Yobale, whose husband, Bula, is of the same subclan section as Kaupa. *Komiti* Degago first heard the case at the hamlet of Baume. Everyone thought the case had been concluded when Kaupa insulted Yobale and the case was reopened and brought to Council Sago at Mul. As I observed only the moot in Mul, I will present only the dialogue from that portion of the case. However, the disputants do describe the events that transpired earlier.

Dialogue

Yobale: At night, I was sleeping. I heard something at the door and went to let the dog out, but there was a man in my house. I was startled, but he told me not to be afraid. I added wood to the fire and sat down on the other side of the room but did not talk. He asked if I had any sweet potatoes because he was hungry. I said I did not. I had eaten some vegetables and gone to sleep. I had some sweet potatoes, but wanted to bring them to sell at the market the next day. Kaupa said that he would give me two kina and, when I go to the market, I could buy sugar and tinned milk for him and I could keep the extra. I took the two kina and went to sleep. Kaupa said he would leave, but if he felt cold, he would come back again. He went out and I closed the door, but I had no lock. He left and I went to sleep. Later, I heard the door open; I thought it was the dog again, but Kaupa was back at the fire. He put his hands out and held my arm and leg. I pulled away, and he ran out. I saw his face and now I have come to tell everyone.

Kaupa: One time, a teacher from Salt/Nomane came to Mul and we sat down together. I sold him some coffee and got money. I gave some to some women and children. A man from Gumine had been engaged to a Kuri Nera woman, but she did not like him so they were going to give back the pay, and I went to watch and listen. I went over to another Malaku men's house and played cards. My brother came later and, after we finished there, we went over to one of the Gui Gaulin men's houses. After playing cards there, we went back to the other men's house. Rafael cooked some food. Gel and Gekabe came up and we told them we were waiting to eat. So we just sat a while. Rafael gave me two kina. We left and went to Baune. Gel had a lamp, so I said we should walk over to Gaulima and play cards there. Gel had not eaten yet, so he went to eat, and my brother and I went to Yobale's house. My brother went in first, got a blanket, and went off to sleep. Then I went inside and asked for sweet potatoes. Yobale said she did not have any. I had lost thirteen kina playing cards. I left and went to Gaulima to watch them play dice. I wanted to play but there was no room for me. I was tired of standing so I went to sleep on a bed. I got up in the morning and left.

Yobale said I came in twice, but I did not come back the second time. At eight o'clock I went to Gaulima and did not come back. I lost all of my money except for the two kina that I had given to Yobale. I asked her to buy the food for me, and I left.

Yobale: You came later; at eleven or twelve o'clock because the radio was finished. I saw your face—I am not lying. You came after I was sleeping.

Kaupa: You are not telling the truth. Before, you did not give times. Now you heard me and you are saying times. You are lying, just following my talk.

Yobale: What are you thinking? That is not your house, it belongs to my husband. My husband went to Mt. Hagen and I was there by myself. Why did you come inside? That was wrong.

Komiti Degago: The first time Kaupa came inside, no man was there, only an old woman slept. You did not tell us about the first time Kaupa came in and told you he would come back. You are not talking clear to the *kot*. [His implication is that she should have gone immediately to tell someone that Kaupa said he was coming back.] Before, when we were talking about this, you did not give us the whole story. I do not like this.

Kaupa: She did not talk clearly. She just followed what I said.

Yobale: Before, we finished this on top at Baune and Kaupa gave me two kina, but then he began to talk crossly to me. He told me that I was not good-looking or fat. He said that I am skinny like a chicken.

Tia Kumal (Yobale's husband's father): So what if that is true? Why did you talk like that to her? She is a man's daughter, and we do not talk like that to people.

Kaupa: I became angry because she spoke crossly to me. I told her that I had helped to pay the bride price for her and asked her why she was talking like that to me. She asked why I tried to fool around with her. I said that I had not and that I had helped buy her. Then I became angry and spoke crossly to her.

[Komiti Degago repeats each story and points out that they do not mesh and that someone is lying. Yobale says that she wants four kina and not two kina as compensation. Council Sago, who has thus far not said a word, is holding the two kina previously given.]

Komiti Degago: If I had four kina, I would give it to her, but I do not. I gave two kina to Council Sago to give to Yobale because Kaupa has no money.

Kaupa: I did not break the door as she says. Mal Waia sat on it and broke it before. They did not put it back well so it fell down by itself.

Council Sago: Did you see Kaupa's face? Do not lie.

Yobale: Yes, it is true, I am not lying.

Council Sago (to Kaupa): Did you hear the woman call out for the men to come look at the intruder?

Kaupa: No, because I was at Gaulima.

Council Sago: Did the Malaku people see you?

Kaupa: Yes, they all saw me. I slept there until dawn.

Council Sago: We do not know who is telling the truth. Kaupa did not really "steal" her, so this is really a *kot* over nothing.

Wemen: I'm thinking of the broken door, and I think you should give her four kina.

[The moot proceeds for an additional thirty minutes, with various parties repeating the same story of what had gone on until finally Wemen shifts the argument.]

Wemen: He did not really "steal" her, but the law of the government says that when her man is away, other men cannot go into a woman's house. You went in and gave her two kina, so you broke the law. Give her four kina.

Council Sago: Yobale, do not be cross with me. The stories are conflicting, and I do not know whom to believe. Besides, Kaupa did not really "steal" you.

Yobale: If it was just that, I would take the two kina. But he spoke crossly to me. I want two kina for that—four kina all together.

Council Sago: We do not know about the broken door or Kaupa coming inside, but he did call you skin and bones, so four kina is all right.

[The moot breaks up with Kaupa saying that he will try to find two kina more and give it to Yobale that afternoon.]

This case is an example of a conflict of fact; that is, did Kaupa break the door and enter Yobale's house the second time? Though it would seem to be a simple matter of calling witnesses from Gaulima to ascertain whether Kaupa had slept there all night, this was not done. Instead, the case was maneuvered so that these issues became secondary. It was, in fact, known that Kaupa had gone into the house on the first occasion (while her husband was away) and that he had called Yobale skinny during the moot. On these grounds Kaupa found it acceptable to make a small compensatory payment. Yobale, at the same time, received payment for both offenses. By maneuvering the issues in this fashion, the councilor and *komiti* provided an avenue through which the dispute could be concluded without further injury to ongoing social relations.

The final case of adultery involves disputants who are members of the same subclan of the Egaku clan but different sections, Boi and Kumaima. After the grievance became known, the two groups readied spears and bows and arrows, but Council Kora was able to convince both sides to hold a moot the following day. As I have suggested above, greater social distance corresponds to a greater likelihood of escalation. In this case the issue was compounded by a history of hostile relations between the disputants' respective groups. The moot itself lasted for over three hours and included two brief cooling-off periods of approximately one-half hour each. The dialogue was often hostile, and frequently groups of men were shouting at the same time. For this reason, a full transcription of the case was not possible and what I do have is too lengthy to detail.

Two previous events made for increased hostility during the present case. Both were brought up repeatedly during the moot.

About thirty years ago, it was reported, a large fight occurred between the Egaku clan and the Keriwiwiku clan of Deri. The trouble began between members of the Boi subclan section and the Keriwiwikus, though no one recalls the reason. During the fighting none of the Bois were killed, but many of the Kumaimas died

During disputes men and women gather to hear the discussion and to comment on the merits of the case. Percentagewise, one is far more likely to find men than women at dispute gatherings.

helping the Bois. Late one night, the Keriwiwikus came and blocked the door of a large Kumaima men's house and then set it ablaze. "All the Kumaimas died, but a few got away [sic]. They went around and slept in women's houses or in pig's houses." In the meantime, the Bois prospered. When Europeans came, the Kumaimas began to grow in number and are now a large group once again. However, they remember that many died helping the Bois and no compensation was given to them for their losses. All agree that this is the reason why now, when any small trouble comes up between member of the two groups, they are ready to fight.

The second issue aggravating the relations between the two groups was a recent case of adultery. In this instance, a Kumaima man committed adultery with the wife of a man from Boi. It could not be settled at a moot so the man was brought to the police station. He was tried in court and sentenced to jail. The issue that remains, according to the Kumaimas, is that he is now out of jail but has not yet given them any compensation. Viewed from the other side, offenders who pay compensation and go to jail often feel they have been doubly punished. Kambu, Lagogo, Dawekai, and Townadong (1974) note, that in such instances occurring in other parts of the Simbu Province, an individual may demand the return of some of his compensation payment, and the refusal to do so may result in fighting.

CASE 10—THE MORNING AFTER ADULTERY

On Saturday night, May 5, 1977, a small party was held to celebrate the completion of a house that one of the most important men of the Malaku clan,

Ninkama, had built for one of his daughters. Milike and his wife, Ana, of the Boi subclan section attended, as did Boi of the Kumaima section. [Both are members of the Egaku clan and Kobula subclan.] Much beer was consumed. Some time during the evening Ana and Boi went off together. The following morning Ana told her husband what had happened and asked if he would bring a case against Boi. Milike said that he would not, thinking Boi had been only fooling around. But Ana was insistent and explained the details of what had gone on. That night the two groups were close to fighting when Council Kora, who is a Kumaima, convinced them that they should try to straighten things out at a moot the following day.

As soon as the trouble came to the surface, the Kumaimas sent forty kina to the Bois, but the Bois returned the money, saying, "What is that? We buy rice for forty kina and eat it in one day."

A moot was convened the following day. Council Kora's opening remarks indicate the hostility and potentiality of violence in this case.

Council Kora: All you men must stand far apart. Bois on one side and Kumaimas on the other and I will stand in the middle. You old men and young ones know that now we have laws. Things like this do not lead to fighting. Fighting is a rubbish custom. Now we have good times and must all sit down quietly together. When any small trouble came up between these two groups, it became a big thing. Now you from Boi must decide what you want for compensation, and we must give it to you. Now we can try to settle this and give compensation. If we cannot, we will have to go to the patrol officer in Guimine. This will double the trouble, and we should be able to settle it ourselves. You two groups should not think that I am on one side or the other. I stand in the middle. You cannot think badly of me. Now let us start.

You must all talk easy back and forth and give some pay so that we can straighten this out. Last night I heard that people were ready to fight. Now I have come and we can settle this. You older men, do not try to incite the young men to fight. If all the young men fight, they will get bloody noses and their noses will swell up.

On Sunday [sic], we all went to Ninkama's house and drank plenty of beer. That night Boi began to fool around with Milike's wife, Ana. That night they went home and in the morning Ana told Milike what had happened and asked him if he would *kot* Boi or not.

I am very cross with this woman. When the man began to fool around with her she should have told him to go away—that she is married to one of his "brothers." Or she could have gone to Ninkama or Milike and they could have held a moot right away. Instead, she fooled around with Boi and then told her husband in the morning.

Both sides agreed with Council Kora that Ana had not acted properly. Some on each side pointed out that they must forget the past and that now is the time of moots, not fighting. They also emphasized that they are one *lain* [clan], in this context meaning members of the same subclan. Others, however, persisted in bringing up the two grievances described above. The members of the Boi section reported that they were also upset because the councilor and all of the *komitis* are members of the Kumaima section and the Bois have no councilor or *komitis* in their section. As a result, they felt they did not have a fair chance.

After hours of heated discussion, the two sections agreed that the payment of a pig would be acceptable. A medium-sized pig [valued at about K 150–K 200] was brought, killed, and given to Milike. Several of the men from Boi were upset because they had not been given the opportunity to examine the pig before it was killed, while others were happy because the case was over. One of the Kumaimas put ten kina on top of the dead pig, saying that he was happy the case was finished. However, others began shouting that Boi [the individual] can no longer come in Boi clan territory, even though some of his gardens are there. The Kumaimas responded that the Bois could not start that kind of trouble, and the two sides argued back and forth. Shortly thereafter, the moot broke up.

During the moot few words were heard from either of the two original disputants. The structural distance between them allowed for expansion into a conflict between the groups, which in this case was specifically related to past grievances that had not been settled by the payment of compensation.

By referring to the two groups as "one-blood" at several points during the moot, Council Kora highlighted the fact that, though they are separate sections, they are members of the same subclan and should, therefore, try to avoid fighting. He also pointed out that the laws of the government and of the church both forbid fighting. Although peace was maintained and Milike may have felt satisfied, the larger issue of intergroup hostility was not resolved.

LAND ENCROACHMENT

Land encroachment was the central issue in only four cases (6.2%). In the densely populated Marigl Valley, land may certainly be considered a scarce resource. This is reflected in the tenacity with which people hold on to, and dispute over, land. In three of the four cases, violence was the first choice of action. The lone case in which violence was not used involved siblings quarreling over a coffee garden.

Attempts to encroach upon another's land can be seen as a blow to a man's prestige. More important, however, is that the reduction of a man's land holdings reduces his productive capacity and also his capacity to raise pigs. This has the long-range effect of a reduction of his prestige and that of his heirs. If the encroacher is from outside the group, this results in lowering the overall productive capacity of the group and will, in the long run, affect their prestige. Thus, encroachment by an outsider may expand into a group concern. This, I believe, results in the pattern revealed in table 6-6.

There are two explanations that, I believe, account for the high proportion of these conflicts within the subclan section. The first, and more sociological, explana-

TABLE 6-6   LAND ENCROACHMENT CLASSIFIED BY STRUCTURAL DISTANCE

Structural Distance	N	%
Same subclan section	3	75
Same subclan/different section	0	0
Same clan/different subclan	0	0
Same tribe/different clan	1	25
Different tribe	0	0
Total	4	100

tion is analogous to that used to explain a similar distribution of adultery cases: fear of the expansion of individual disputes into group conflict mitigates against the culturally approved action of encroachment on the land of outsiders, while the resolvability of such disputes between insiders, which is culturally disapproved, allows such actions to occur with less threat of expansion into warfare.

The second explanation suggests the fairly obvious solution that the frequency of cases is related to the distribution of land holdings. The logical extension of the distribution of land ownership described in chapter 2 is that there will be fewer common borders between members of different tribes than between members of different clans within the tribe. There will be more common borders between members of the subclan than between individuals who are members of the same clan but different subclans. The greatest number of common borders are between members of the same subclan section. Thus, one could say that structural distance is inversely related to the frequency of common property borders.

Certainly, it is far easier for mistakes to occur in marking borders between adjacent lands than between nonadjacent lands; and, almost as certainly, it is far more simple to encroach a few feet into a neighbor's land while his garden is under fallow cover than it is to encroach upon land not adjacent to one's own. This, in fact, is exactly what appears to have happened in the case which follows.

CASE 11—NEIGHBORLY LAND ENCROACHMENT

On April 2, 1977, a land dispute erupted between Garami and Kaupa, both of the Kobula Gaulin subclan section of the Kun Kora clan [Kunaraku]. The ground in question was a long strip about eight feet wide, lying on the border between the gardens of the two men.

Garami claimed that the land was his and had belonged to his father's father and that Kaupa had moved the marker while planting his own garden. Kaupa replied that his father had planted a garden on this ground and that it therefore belonged to him.

The argument became heated and the two men began to fight. The fight ended when Garami was injured. The men called out for *Komiti* Sine of the Maima Gaulin subclan section since their own section had no councilor or *komiti*.

A moot was convened by *Komiti* Sine. He argued that the ground was not important but that Garami and Kaupa were of one blood and should not fight. He suggested dividing the ground so that each man would have a strip four feet wide. This was accepted. Kaupa also paid an additional six kina to Garami to compensate for his injury. The two men shook hands and left.

During the moot, *Komiti* Sine emphasized the importance of the relations between the disputants over the value of the ground. The injury incurred during the fight was brought up as a separate grievance and compensation was paid without regard to whose fault the fight had been. This two-part settlement—that is, splitting the ground and paying compensation—was the best possible alternative for restoring ruptured social relations. To have given the ground to either party would have risked creating lasting enmity between the two men.

CASE 12—THE CASE OF THE FIGHTING OLD MEN

On April 2, 1977, Koma Sago (Naraku clan, Kune subclan, Dabile subclan section; see also cases 4, 5, and 6) began the construction of a new house for his wife on ground that, as it turned out, belonged to Sine, a member of the same one-blood group as Koma.

Early on the morning of April 5, Sine and his brother Gui came down the mountain from their men's house at Baune. Without warning, the two brothers attacked Koma's father, old Sago, who was sitting on the ground in front of his men's house in the Mul ceremonial ground. Using staffs six to eight feet long and over two inches thick, Sine and Gui attacked old Sago, who was hit on the head, arm, and finger before he was able to get up and defend himself. The three old men fought as bystanders attempted to break them apart. People were at last able to disarm the three fighters, but occasionally one would grab a staff and run toward his opponent. I noted, however, that though Gui had an axe in his belt, he would run for a staff rather than draw his axe.

Council Sago, a member of the same men's house as old Sago, was extremely upset and torn between retaliation and the "proper" behavior for a leader and councilor.

When I inquired into why Sine and Gui had attacked old Sago rather than Koma, I was told that it was because "he should have taught his son better," that is, not to build a house on someone else's land without asking permission first.

Since Koma was out working in his garden at the time, there was a delay while we waited for him to arrive at the ceremonial ground. During this time Sine added insult to injury by herding pigs onto the site where Koma had been working on the house. At last Koma arrived, looking extremely cross and carrying his axe, bush knife, and a long sapling. He walked directly past Sine without a word. When he reached the ceremonial ground where most of the men were gathered, he quickly fashioned a fighting staff out of the sapling. This was a symbolic gesture, since bystanders were easily able to restrain Koma.

By this point it was clear that the issue had shifted from one of land, which no one had contested because it was common knowledge that the ground did, indeed, belong to Sine, to one of physical injury. Although Koma had been physically restrained, the situation remained tense as verbal abuse continued between Sine and Gui [who occasionally had to be physically restrained] on the one hand, and old Sago, Koma, and Council Sago, on the other.

Seeing no movement toward settlement, old Sago's younger son, Kuria, took his father to the police station at Gumine. Shortly after they had left, a few men called after them not to go to the police ["to put Sine in jail"], saying that Sine would give old Sago a chicken. Kuria and old Sago later reported to me that they had not heard these invocations.

With old Sago gone, the crowd dispersed and Council Sago took time out to handle a moot involving pig damage to some sugar cane. When that case was concluded, he left for the government station where the present case was to be continued.

At first Sine did not appear at the police station, but finally Council Maima of the Malaku clan showed up with Sine, though his brother Gui remained in Mul [he later told me that he had not come to Gumine because he was afraid of being put in jail]. The two councilors from Mul, Sago and Maima; the disputants, Sine and old Sago; as well as Koma and Kuria, were joined by ex-*luluai* Dai from Gumine. These men sat on the ground about twenty-five yards from the police station. Interested onlookers from Mul or Gumine stood by watching but rarely made comment. The seating arrangement of the councilors and disputants reveals the shift of the issue under dispute from one between Sine and Koma over land to one between Sine and old Sago over physical injury.

After the disputants arrived at the government station, the case was reported to the police. The police suggested that since Sine was an old man and jail would be detrimental to his health, the councilors should settle matters on their own. Settling the dispute outside the police station, as well as the hour-long walk from Mul to the government station, which provided a cooling-off period, assured that violence would not erupt during this stage of dispute processing.

Dialogue

Council Sago: I was not at the men's house, but at my wife's house. I heard the fighting, so I ran to look. Sine and Gui were hitting old Sago. I was sorry for the old man and so I told them, "That's enough. The old man did not build the house, his son did." I got angry, Koma came down, and now we have come to the police station.

I brought old Sago to the police station [sic], but the others were "big-heads" and stayed at Mul. All right, now Sine has come, though Gui has not, and we can straighten it out.

Council Maima: Gui did not come. All right, we can straighten it anyway and then go back to Mul.

Two men joined together and beat up one man. If you had broken his head altogether, you would have to run to the police station. Now, you just scraped his head, so we can straighten it. Now, I have brought Sine, but he is an old man. It will not be good if they put him in jail, so we can straighten it outside the police station.

If young men and middle-age men fight, that is all right, but not old men. If they get put in jail, people from all around will be ashamed and ask why we could not "straighten it" ourselves.

Council Sago: All right, I was at my wife's house. I saw them come down and hit him hard. I saw it. Old Sago got a stick and went to fight back. Many young men broke up the fight. Maima did not see the beginning, I did. I will talk clearly so that you can "straighten" things out at this moot.

Council Maima: I think that Council Sago came first with old Sago and that you would like to put Sine in jail. Sine thinks the same. Council Sago should have straightened it at Mul and not come to the police station. Now we can straighten it outside the police station and then go back to Mul.

The law of the court is that we must all come to the police station. If we are friendly about it, the police are happy. But, if half the people stay at Mul, angry, that is not good.

Council Sago: True, we came first and Sine and Gui stayed at Mul, so it is hard work. But now Sine has come and we can straighten it.

Koma: I was building my house and went to the bush to get more materials early in the morning. Sine and Gui should have asked where I was, and when I came back they could have fought with me or held a moot. But they should not have beaten up my father. I could break their heads, too.

It is hard work to find wood for the house, so I had to go a long way. I began to build the house and Simon [Sine's son] came. I asked Simon if I could build the house there, and he said that it was all right. Now the two men come down angry! Simon thought that the ground was red and not good anyway. If I put a house there, the ground will be good later and they can put a garden there. So Simon said that it was all right for me to build a house there.

Ex-luluai Dai   (to Sine): You do not think. On red ground you must cook food, and so forth. Then the ground will become good and you will be able to grow food on it.

Old Sago: Many times I have given them pigs, large mother of pearl shells, and all kinds of things. They did not give them back to me. Now they all come and fight with me. Now they must go find plenty of money and pigs to give to me. I do not want a little chicken. You must give me something big.

Early in the morning I heard them talking angrily about me on top [of the mountain at Baune], but I did not yell back. Then they came down and fought with me. I am older than Sine. When he was a little boy, I looked out for him well, like his brother. I used to give him food and so he grew up big. Now he is too old and too proud, so he comes and fights with me.

Council Sago: That is all true. Now you are old men and we must straighten this.

Ex-luluai Dai   (asks Old Sago): He is like your brother. He is an old man now, too. Do you want to put him in jail, or do you want payment?

Old Sago: He is old. It is not good if I put him in jail. He will die. He can give me payment, and I can take it.

Koma: I had to work hard to get wood to build this house, and I am angry now. If I was there I could have fought with them. But I was out in the bush. After they beat up my father, I was called back and so I came. I broke a stick [made a fighting staff]. I wanted to hit them, but Council Sago and the others said I should not break the law, so I dropped my stick. Now Gui and Sine must give pay to my father.

Council Sago: All right, this is something just between us. Let us straighten it and go home.

Ex-luluai Dai: Sine, you do not know what it is like in jail. You stay only at your place. Now you and Gui go home with your children, who are big now, collect money and give it to old Sago. Before [during the time before independence], when people were put in jail they got good food. Now they do not get good food. If you go into jail on Monday, then Monday, Tuesday, Wednesday, Thursday, Friday, and Saturday, you sleep without eating. It is not good; your stomach will break and you will die. You had better run to your place and gather up pay and give it to old Sago.

Sine: In the morning I sang out and then came down [from Baune to Mul]. I asked whether Koma was here or not. One young man yelled "shut up," so I got very angry. Gui and I ran down. We looked for Koma, but he was not there. Gui got a stick and ran down. He did not really hit him but merely threatened him twice. So I made a fighting staff and came down and hit old Sago. The old man said, angrily, that it was not good ground. He said "the good ground is still there. This ground is red. Why are you so angry over this ground of yours?" I got angry and hit him twice on the head, the third time on the hand, which brought blood. This is all. We did not talk much.

Ex-luluai Dai: You are good for bringing out the root of how it happened. It is good that you talk straight.

Sine: It is true. I hit my number-one brother. I am number two. I will go back and get one chicken. I will kill it, cook it in a saucepan, and give it to old Sago.

Old Sago: If you kill it and give it to me, I will not eat it. Give me a live one and I will care for it.

Sine: All right, I will give you one chicken and six kina as well. You can take it. We are not outsiders. We are "brothers." I have hit you, so I can give you a little payment. I hit you and drew blood. You went to hit me, but all the men came and held us back so you did not hit me.

Ex-luluai Dai: You are not outsiders, but "brothers" fighting. You can go to Mul and give him some money and a chicken. It is up to you and the councilors to straighten it at Mul.

Old Sago: If he gives me a live chicken and some money it will be all right.

Council Maima: All right, Council Sago and I have come to hear this. Dai has "straightened" it and it is over. [Council Maima takes out two kina of his own and puts it in Sine's net bag.] I am giving you two kina to help you. Now I am like the Member of Parliament [i.e., a very important man]. Now, you all see me give two kina to Sine. None of you do that, but I have good ways, so I do it.

Ex-luluai Dai: Oh, that is a very good way! Now you give two kina to Sine to help him make the compensation payment. You put it in Sine's net bag.

Wemen: Koma went to the bush. I was with old Sago when the two men came and hit him. Gui and Sine and their children must pay old Sago.

Koma: The talk is over. Let us go finish it at Mul.

Sine: Wemen, why are you talking? This is between my "brother" and me.

Wemen: He is a very old man. You must give him plenty of money. Buy some fish and rice, cook it, and we can sit down and it will be over.

Simon: Wemen, you are nothing. Me too. I own the ground but I am nothing. We did not fight, only them. It is something between them. We should not interfere.

Council Poi   (Kunaraku): It is over now. Go get the chicken and some money and give it to the old man. Now you all go.

[At this point all parties returned to Mul. Two days later, Sine and Gui gave a chicken and six kina to old Sago.]

In this case we see that even close kinsmen, members of the same one-blood group, make use of violence when their land holdings appear to be threatened. The most striking aspect of this case, however, is that after the initial attack, the issue of the land encroachment is almost completely dropped and replaced by the issue of physical injury. Once it was brought to public attention, everyone knew that Koma should have asked Sine before beginning construction of a house on Sine's land. With regard to the original grievance, Sine was the offended party. However, his resort to violence, which resulted in injury (though minor) to old Sago, created a new grievance and caused a shift in roles; Sine became the offender and old Sago became the offended party.

The scene that took place at the Mul ceremonial ground, and that brought Sine's displeasure over Koma's encroachment to public notice, was one of open violent hostility. After the initial fighting, the disputants were physically restrained. Nevertheless, there was tension in the air, and I felt as though renewed fighting might erupt at any moment. Bringing the disputants to the police and holding the discussion in front of the police station substantially reduced the potentiality of violent confrontation during the moot. The police and the councilors agreed that old men should not be put in jail and, as a result, the police advised the councilors to handle it themselves rather than forwarding the case to criminal court.

Over two months after receiving the chicken and the six kina, old Sago was still upset with Sine and Gui, though superficially they were able to interact in public. Despite the seriousness of the case, few persons outside the immediate families took an active part in the proceedings. The dispute did not result in animosity between groups or the creation of factions within the subclan section. It was, rather, attributed to "the ways of old men."

DOMESTIC CONFLICT

Marital disputes and disputes between co-wives usually remain within the nuclear family, though occasionally a third party may, informally, offer advice or aid. It is difficult in a dispersed community to obtain an adequate sample of conflicts between husbands and wives. I suspect that the four cases (6.2% of all cases) reported here do not represent the actual frequency of this type of conflict as compared to the other categories of grievance.

In the following case, the grievance situation is such that the dispute expands into an issue between the husband's group and that of the wife.

CASE 13—THE RAGE OF HUI KORA

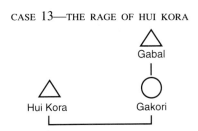

Hui Kora, a man from the Keriwiwiku clan from Deri, is married to Gakori, who was born into the Egaku clan, Maima subclan, and Kobulamable subclan section of the Kobulaku tribe. After they had been married a short time, Gakori's younger brother came to stay with her.

On the morning of May 6, 1977, an argument occurred between Hui Kora and Gakori. Hui had come to his wife's house expecting breakfast, but it had not yet been prepared. He told Gakori that she must rise early, cook his food, and then go to work in the garden. When Gakori explained that she had just awoken, Hui became angry and struck her. She went off to work in the garden.

But Hui was still angry and, in a fit of rage, set fire to his wife's house. Little did he realize that his wife's brother was still sleeping inside. While in her garden, Gakori saw the smoke rising from her house. She called out to the men and they all ran to see what they could do. Fortunately, they were able to break down the door and rescue the child.

The people from the Maima Gaulin subclan were extremely upset over the threat to the child's life. They said that in the past they fought with the Keriwiwikus and the Keriwiwikus had burnt many of their houses and killed many of their people. Now that they are trying to raise a new generation of children, they said, the Keriwiwikus are trying to burn them in their houses again. They got ready to fight. The Maimas were restrained by the words of Council Kora. Two weeks later a moot was convened, with Gabal [the boy's father] bringing the action against his daughter's husband, Hui Kora.

During the moot the argument became heated, but all ended well because of Hui Kora's generosity. Hui said that he had not known that the child was inside, and he admitted that he had broken the law of the government [as understood by the community members]. As compensation, he gave a large pig, forty kina, and a goat.

Gabal and the other Maima Gaulins were pleased with the payment because, as they said, Hui Kora gave a big payment, despite the fact that the child had not died.

The initial dispute was over Gakori's failure to cook Hui's breakfast. However, in this case, as in others that have already been presented, violence (in the form of burning Gakori's house) precipitated a new grievance (the near injury to her brother). The new grievance then became the central issue of dispute. The conflict was further compounded by the past relations of enmity existing between the groups to which the two disputants (Hui Kora and Gabal) belonged. Although the dispute did expand into the concern of the two groups, in this case, unlike the case of adultery (case 10) described above, the new grievance and the particular disputants remained as the central focus.

The size of the compensation payment made by Hui Kora to his wife's father indicates his concern with maintaining harmonious ongoing social relations. His admission of guilt and his generous compensation payment did as much to raise his own status in the eyes of the Maima Gaulins as obstinacy would have done to lower it. Here again, we see that it is generosity and a willingness to pay up quickly, rather than compromise, which served to restore a valuable social relationship.

The five categories of grievance discussed in this chapter account for 85 percent of the sixty-five cases collected in the field. The remaining ten cases are distributed over six categories of offense. Four of these categories contain only one case each. The categories of insult (four cases) and disputes over children (two cases) contain grievances that are so diverse as to make the comparison of cases, and, therefore, generalization within these categories, meaningless.

CONCLUSION

The data presented in this chapter suggest that people's decisions about how to handle a grievance, as well as the overall behavior of disputants during conflict, are related to four aspects of the grievance situation. The first, and probably the most important, criterion is the type of grievance itself. Despite assertions to the contrary by a long line of scholars, I believe that the nature of the offense plays an important role in how people handle troubled cases. Land encroachment, for example, is an issue quite different from garden damage. Other factors being equal, this affects individual behaviors in conflict management.

The second criterion is the structural distance between the disputants. Structural distance is inversely related to the desire for settlement. Disputants who are members of different tribes have less interest in restoring social relations than do members of the same one-blood group. This affects dispute behavior.

The third criterion is the past history of relations between the individual disputants. People do not live in a historical void. Individual behaviors affect and redefine relationships. Past relations of cooperation or conflict affect present-day understandings of a situation as well as behavioral responses to an offense.

The fourth and final criterion is the past history of relations between the groups to which the disputants are affiliated. A history of enmity between groups may result in the expansion of conflict. Good relations, on the other hand, give reason for settlement.

These four factors are the criteria that define the grievance situation and, thereby, influence decisions and actions that result from them. There may, indeed, be other criteria. At this point, however, these four emerge from the case materials as the most salient factors influencing individual decision making and, therefore, the distribution of case loads.

These findings help illuminate conflict management in the New Guinea Highlands. But there is something unsatisfying about simplistically linking these structural and historical criteria to actions. It seems that understanding *why* these criteria influence decisions and actions and *how* the criteria interact in response to variations in the grievance situation requires a more fine-grained analysis. In other words, how can we explain the connection between the structural/situational criteria and the decisions/actions? In the next chapter, I employ the concept of goals as a link between these variables.

7 / The Role of Goals in Decision Making and Action

Understanding human society and human behavior is a complex undertaking. We began by examining the social institutions of conflict management—the structure of opportunity—within which each individual operates. We determined that there are a number of situational factors, arising out of social structure or history, that lead to certain types of behavior. At the same time, it seems to me that human behaviors are inextricable from the individual's goals—even when goals, such as increasing power or prestige, may not be consciously recognized. "To say that all human action is directed to the attainment of goals seems obvious and indisputable; indeed, one could argue that goal-orientation is simply a defining quality of action" (Cohen 1968:70).

Suggesting that individual behavior is goal-directed is not to argue against the importance of social structure, history, or norms and values. In the first part of this volume, I examined Simbu culture and society. I reviewed, for example, group organization and the social relations that derive from them, arguing that conflict management must be understood within the broad social and cultural context. In the second part, I looked at conflict management as a social institution. Dyadic and triadic modes of conflict management were described as options which an individual might choose. I described the overall system as a "structure of opportunity" and focused attention on the patterns of action that result from the choices people make during conflict situations. In the previous chapter, I used tables, cases, and figures to examine the disputing process and to identify four decision-making criteria: the nature of the offense, the structural distance between disputants, the history of relations between individuals, and the history of relations between groups.

These structural and situational criteria are independent variables, causally linked to behavior in disputes. For example, individuals that are close kin are more likely to negotiate or mediate with great concern over the maintenance of their relationship, while those who are more distant kin or not kin at all will be less concerned. All other factors being equal, these four factors will tend to determine disputants' behavior. This understanding, however, is rather simplistic.

What is lacking is any sense of interaction between the criteria. While it was necessary to examine each independently in the first stage of analysis, we all know the world doesn't work this way. The type of offense, social structure, and history are all acting at once, pushing or pulling the individual, sometimes in similar directions and sometimes in opposite ones.

My strategy for attaining some form of synthesis is to "elaborate" on the causal relationship between actions and the antecedent structural and situational variables. The term *elaboration,* in social science, refers to a specific use of statistical procedures in which an antecedent or intervening variable (or test factor) is introduced into a two-variable relationship. An antecedent variable is one that comes before a second variable. An intervening variable is one that comes between two variables. The elaboration procedure refines or specifies the causal linkages between the variables.

Take, as a very simple hypothetical example, the relationship between gender and aggression. Even if there is a clear statistical correlation, one may ask how this comes about; that is, what is the mechanism by which maleness leads to aggression? Some may suggest biological explanations and others cultural explanations. In either case, the elaboration process involves the introduction of additional variables, such as socialization. It might be argued that being born male leads to a culturally defined form of socialization that, in turn, leads to increased levels of aggression. The variable "socialization" intervenes between maleness and aggression and thereby helps to explain the relationship. In other words, being born male causes the individual to be treated in certain ways, and this causes differences in aggression between men and women. The next step might be to examine the relationship between gender and socialization. Here one might, for example, examine the environment. In this way, causal chains are built that increasingly refine our knowledge of social process.

I will use the elaboration model, but my argument will be conceptual rather than statistical. If a conceptual framework is found to fit the ethnographic data and if it serves to explain or further the understanding of that data, then the concept has utility. It is in terms of utility for the advancement of knowledge that concepts (and definitions) are judged (Hemple 1952:47; Phillips 1971:39–61; Pelto 1970: 10–11).

Begin by viewing the relation between the grievance situation and actions as causal. The structural and situational criteria that define the grievance situation are antecedent and causally related to the decisions that lead to actions. What variable or concept can be introduced to explain the relationship between the grievance situation (and each of the defining criteria) and actions? I suspect the reader will not be surprised when I suggest concept of goals.

The interpretation of figure 7-1 is as follows: at time A, an individual finds himself or herself in a grievance situation. The criteria that define the grievance situation are assessed, resulting in decisions regarding goals; that is, the disputant decides what he or she wants. As a result, disputants decide on what they perceive

Figure 7-1   The Intervening Variable: Goals

as the best means of attaining their goals (a strategy). Implementing these decisions results in observable actions. What we see is the grievance and the actions. What we assume is that those actions are consciously or unconsciously goal-directed.

> Sine thought she would get her day's chores done early. So it was daybreak when she headed out through the brisk mountain air to her garden. She hadn't anticipated finding Gui's hungry hog feasting on her ripe sweet potatoes. But there he was. What should shedo? Should she shoo the pig out of the garden to save the remaining crops or should she let him stay so others could see whose pig had damaged her garden? How much damage had been done? Of course, Gui is a member of her husband's one-blood group and nothing like this had ever happened before, so she was sure there would be little problem. So off she went to get her husband, Koma, and together they went to visit Gui. (See case 4.)

At this point Sine and Koma are involved in what I have termed a grievance situation. They assess the situation, set goals, and approach Gui. Setting goals, as we shall see later, may not be easy since some of the factors may suggest one goal while other factors suggest just the opposite. The moment Sine and Koma express their concerns to Gui, a dispute is born. Gui now finds himself in a grievance situation. Like Sine and Koma, he will assess the nature of the dispute, the structural relations between them, and their individual and group histories. In setting goals, he will weigh these criteria.

All disputes are minimally dyadic and can be viewed as a transactional process involving the action and reaction of the disputants. Moreover, each action may redefine the grievance situation. Thus disputing is an ongoing interaction and reevaluation process. In a sense the grievance situation is always changing. One may view dispute processing as an articulation process whereby each action, verbal or nonverbal, adds insight into an opponent's goals. The confirmation that one understands the information being transmitted by one's opponent may be seen as a redefining of the grievance situation. Gulliver (1973) characterizes the negotiation process as one of information and learning.

Figure 7-2 is a model of a two-party dispute transaction. Party I finds himself or herself in a grievance situation. He or she sets goals and takes action. This action communicates a message to the second party. Gui, for example, may have been sitting idly at the ceremonial ground when Sine and Koma approached explaining that Gui's hog had eaten their garden. It is only at this point that Gui finds himself in a grievance situation. The situation includes all the structural and situational criteria

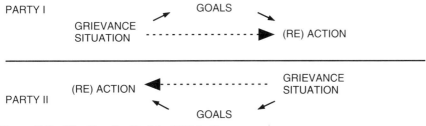

Figure 7-2   The Dyadic Model of Disputing

as well as the message contained in the style of Sine and Koma's communication. Based on his interpretation, he sets goals and acts. This action communicates to Sine and Koma on many levels and may cause them to reevaluate their goals before responding.

Thus the disputing process is a transactional communication process. Through successive rounds, the issues may be contained and conflict reduced or they may expand to include other grievances or other individuals. While disputing involves a communication process, it is important to recognize that it is much more than that. If one understood the communication without understanding the social structure and history, one could not fully comprehend the patterns of behavior.

We may now return to our particular context and show how the concept of goals helps us decipher the relationship between the grievance situation and decisions and actions.

GOALS IN NEW GUINEA DISPUTING

It is obvious to anyone who has observed even a few disputes in contemporary New Guinea Highlands communities that disputants' goals include receiving a satisfactory compensation payment. Compensation looms large in the ethnographic description of Highland societies, and, indeed, compensation was a factor in every case reported in this volume. Recall that the "bottom line," in figure 5-1 (Options for Pursuing a Grievance) asked whether compensation had been paid and whether it was considered sufficient. The function of this payment, according to residents of Mul, is to "make the belly cold" (i.e., abate anger). It is clear, however, that not all payments result in settlement, and it is equally clear that disputants cannot arrive at a settlement without adequate compensation being received.

It would be a serious mistake to view compensation as merely a financial settlement. In fact, I found it impossible to make sense out of the data using the amount of compensation as the dependent variable, that is, to try to predict payments from the other variables. My analysis did, however, indicate that in different situations compensation payments performed different functions. At times financial remuneration was, indeed, a disputant's primary goal, but at other times the compensation payment was only a *means* of attaining more basic goals. Cohen (1968:72) notes that, in general, the attainment of some goals is sometimes a necessary means of attaining others.

Rather than being limited to compensation payments, I find that disputants' goals correspond to three types of restitution.

TYPES OF RESTITUTION

A. The giving or receiving of an equivalent for some loss or damage to property.
B. The restoration of status or prestige.
C. The restoration of all persons to harmony.

Offenders and victims emphasize different aspects of each of these three types of restitution. The goals of the victim, or offended party, in a particular case may be one or a combination of the following: (a) to gain restitution, usually monetary, for the loss of, or damage to, property; (b) to regain prestige lost as a result of the offense; or (c) the restoration of injured social relations.

Similarly, the goal of the offender may be one or a combination of the following: (a) the reduction of the amount of compensation to be paid; (b) the restoration of individual or group prestige, which may have suffered as a result of the offender's own actions (this may sometimes be achieved by securing from the offender a quick and generous compensation payment); or (c) the restoration of injured social relations.

The goals of the disputing parties may be in opposition or they may be complementary. Goal type A, for example, concerns financial restitution. Here the goals of offender and offended would appear to be in opposition. The offended party wants to maximize his or her gain while the offender wants to minimize his or hers. In goal type C, where reestablishing a social relationship is most important, the goals are complementary. Goal type B, having to do with prestige, is more complex. In some situations, the offended party's prestige may have been reduced, while that of the offender's prestige was not affected or may have been raised. In such instances, as in the case of adultery, the goals of the disputants are opposing since the offended party is trying to obtain a substantial payment in order to raise his or her prestige while the offender is trying to reduce the payment. However, in cases where the prestige of both parties has been affected, the goals are complementary. In case thirteen, for example, Hui Kora's quick and generous compensation served to raise the prestige of both parties.

The complexity and interweaving of goals becomes apparent, for example, in cases where monetary restitution is the issue and social relationships are valuable, though not yet disrupted. In such cases, the disputants must press their claims with care, for to do otherwise is to risk a further breach between the disputants. As Cohen (1968:73) notes, "An actor may enter a situation in order to achieve some goal, and may be lead by it to pursue others in addition to, or in place of the original goal." Thus, goals may shift as a result of the disputants' behavior.

Some goals are more highly valued and therefore take priority over others. However, "a rank order of goals may change with changing circumstances" (Cohen 1968:72). Furthermore, "the actor's choice of goals and, in particular, his [or her] ranking of goals, is strongly influenced by norms and values" (Cohen 1968:77). Norms are specific prescriptions and proscriptions of standard behavior. Values express preferences, priorities, or desirable states, but not specific forms of conduct. Following this line reasoning, I argue that disputants evaluate the grievance situation and rank goals according to norms and values of their society, particularly those relating to social structure.

Of course, the actor's knowledge of the situation may be different from the observer's, and it is the actor's knowledge that governs his or her reaction to a situation. The degree of congruence between the actor's and the observer's knowledge of the situation can never be precisely known and, as such, remains problematic in social science research.

In sum, the grievance situation, as *perceived by the actors*, is assessed in terms of norms and values. As a result of this evaluation, individuals prioritize their goals. Once goals are set, actors make decisions leading to behaviors that they perceive as the best means of attaining their goals. Disputants observe the behavior of their opponents, reassess the grievance situation, adjust goals, and take further action. At the theoretical level, each action, indeed the very manner of behavior, modifies, to some degree, the grievance situation and, as a result, reevaluation is an on-going process.

SITUATIONAL CRITERIA AS ISOLATES

I have identified four criteria that define the grievance situation: the type of grievance, the structural distance between the disputants, the past relations between the disputants, and the past relations between the disputants' kin groups. These criteria certainly never act in isolation. In everyday life, one cannot easily separate out the nature of a grievance from the past relations between disputants. If such things were easily separable, we Americans would not so frequently witness minor domestic squabbles expand into homicide cases.

However, to analyze the complex interactive effect, it is necessary to first consider each separately with only a minimum of concern for the effects of the others. In the following sections I will examine how and why each of the four criteria affects the ordering of goal importance by reference to Simbu norms and values.

Type of Grievance

The four major types of grievance—property damage by animals, theft, adulterous behavior, and land encroachment—can be divided into two categories. Grievances over property damage and theft are, in and of themselves, not offensive to the prestige of the injured party or his or her group (except in cases of pig theft). By and large, cases of property damage or theft do not disrupt ongoing social relationships. In these types of cases the victim's goal usually involves financial restitution rather than the restoration of prestige or social relationships.

Grievances over adultery and land encroachment (as well as pig theft) lower the prestige of the victim and may result in an immediate breach in social relations between the disputants. Moreover, if the disputants are members of different groups, the offense may be viewed as an offense against the group. In the case of adulterous behavior, the importance of the relationship between victim and offender determines whether the goal involves only the restoration of prestige, or the repair of ruptured social relations as well. In cases of land encroachment, these factors are compounded by the threat of loss of land. In three out of four land encroachment cases the initial response was violent coercion. As Starr and Yngvesson (1975:560–561) point out, "People who are linked in ongoing relations and who are attempting to gain control over land in a scarcity situation will define themselves as strict adversaries."

Structural Distance

Structural distance is important in two ways. First, the value placed on social solidarity varies inversely with the relative position of the groups in the segmentary system. The smaller the structural distance, the greater the value placed on social solidarity. The ideals of appropriate behavior and the value of maintaining ongoing relations between disputing parties are, therefore, reflected in or measured by the structural distance between the disputants. This may reflect an increasing need for cooperation against outsiders at the lower levels of segmentation. Second, since the members of these groups reside patrilocally, structural closeness corresponds to geographic propinquity. Closer kin tend to live closer together. Structural closeness is associated with the maintenance of multiplex (Gluckman 1955) or mutually valuable (Gulliver 1963) relationships. These sorts of interpersonal relations are distinct from ideals about groups and will be addressed under the heading of relations between individuals.

"Solidarity in any social system may derive from interests that stem from internal social relations" (Cohen 1968:135). Breaches between members of a social group threaten the ongoing social relationships and the solidarity of the group. It follows that maintaining social relations is of paramount importance for the continuity of the group.

I have noted that the structure of groups conforms to a segmentary nesting pattern. Members of the smallest groups conceive of themselves as brothers and as being of one blood. Norms of behavior and the value placed on maintaining relationships correspond to these beliefs. When fights do occur within these smaller groups, weapons are restricted to fists or sticks. The use of lethal weapons, such as axes, spears, or bows and arrows, is prohibited. Frequently, men from the same one-blood group enclose their gardens within a single fence. They help each other in accumulating the bride price needed when a young man of the group wishes to marry and, conversely, bride price payments for young women are distributed among them. People who are members of different one-blood groups, but members of the same subclan, may, though infrequently, refer to one another as "one-blood" during a dispute. However, group sentiments are far weaker than those of the one-blood group, and fighting with lethal weapons is condoned. As groups become more inclusive, that is, as one moves toward the larger units, the degree of mutual interdependence and mutual aid and affection between members declines. At the highest level, where disputants are members of different tribes, particularly if the tribes are from different regions, disputes occur in a social vacuum, though in some instance mitigated by a network of matrilateral and affinal ties (see Podolefsky 1984). I am reminded here of Barbara Yngvesson's (1976:369) conclusions about an Atlantic fishing community:

In contrast to the rules for handling grievance behavior within the bounds of an ongoing relationship, grievance encounters across such boundaries occur within the context of an entirely different set of rules for behavior: (1) The act of grievance occurs in what might be called a social vacuum. . . . Reactions to the grievance need only involve a consideration of its immediate effects and not the repercussions of the act in a field of enduring social relations. The grievance encounter itself may have no past, present, or future, or if it does involve a historical dimension, maintenance of the relationship in the future is not of concern.

History of Relations Between Individuals

The importance of a social relationship affects how people interact in conflict situations. In general, structural closeness is directly associated with the value placed on social ties. Exchange partners, matrilateral ties, or affinal relatives place high value on good relations. There are also individuals who maintain highly valued relations of friendship, making occasional loans of land for garden use or aiding one another in the construction of fences or other labor even though they may be members of different groups. One may wish, however, to distinguish those relations that are backed by cultural values relating to group solidarity from those that arise out of transactions between individuals in terms of goods and services (e.g., mutual aid in garden preparation). Moreover, it is useful to distinguish between more and less highly valued relationships within each category of structural distance.

The impact of past relations can best be understood as a modifier of structural distance. Yngvesson (1976:367) points out that behavior may determine social identity. Though I would not go so far in the New Guinea context, I do agree that repeated cooperation between outsiders or breaches between insiders may serve to redefine a relationship as either more or less valuable than would be expected on the basis of structural distance alone. As such, goal orientation is affected.

The three cases of the hungry hog (cases 4, 5 and 6), presented in chapter 6, reveal the changing attitude of the offended party, Koma, as the result of a series of grievances involving a member of his own one-blood group. In all three cases, the same pig damaged crops in the same garden. In the first two cases, Sine, Koma, and Gui easily determined an appropriate financial restitution and there was no breach of social relations. When the pig went into the garden for the third time, however, it became obvious that Gui, the pig's owner, was not looking out for the property of his "brother," Koma, in the expected fashion, for it is well known that pigs return to areas where they remember having previously feasted. Koma's perception of the grievance situation was modified by this history, and his ranking of goal importance shifted.

History of Relations Between Groups

Norms of social behavior are generally circumscribed as cooperative and harmonious between insiders and competitive between outsiders. However, with the exception of co-members of the same subclan section, these classifications (insider/outsider) are optative. That is, disputants may choose to think of each other as co-members of the larger inclusive group ("we are members of the same tribe") or as members of the opposing smaller groups ("we are members of different clans").

Offenses committed against a member of the group by an outsider may be seen as an offense against the group as a whole, and, concomitantly, the offenders group may be held liable, as a collectivity, for the offensive actions committed by the individual. When this occurs, the dispute may expand from a dispute between individuals to a confrontation between groups. This is a necessary prerequisite to warfare, but not all disputes that expand lead to war. In fact, not all disputes between members of different groups expand. As Moore (1972:97) notes, expansion is "a *potentiality* within certain social situations rather than an inevitable rule governed by the relative social positions of the parties, or the subject of the dispute."

As seen in case 10 over adultery, disputes between individuals provide an opportunity for social groups to bring to the surface long-standing animosities that arise out of past grievances and that have nothing in common with the specific issues at hand. In this particular case, little emphasis was placed on the restoration of social relations despite the fact that the disputants were members of the same subclan. Rather, emphasis was placed on the opposition of sections and on gaining a large compensation payment, a pig, which would have the effect of restoring the prestige of the offended husband and his social group.

GOALS, DECISIONS, AND ACTIONS

We have long known that norms regarding dispute processing, even in areas where they are made explicit, cannot predict human behavior in any simple way (Comaroff and Roberts 1977). The lack of predictable outcomes and behaviors indicates the underlying complexity of the situational criteria and the goals that derive from them.

I have argued that the disputants' goals may be either opposing or complementary. If, based on the situational criteria, both disputants are seeking to restore a social relationship, then their goals are complementary. If one disputant is seeking the highest possible financial settlement and the other seeks to make the lowest possible payment, then the goals are opposing.

In a similar fashion, each *individual* disputant defines his or her goals based on the particular configuration of situational criteria in a given case. We have seen how the criteria in isolation affect goals. The disputants, however, cannot act on the criteria one at a time. He or she views the situation globally. The criteria may suggest goals that are opposing or complementary.

The criteria may be said to be complementary when each directs the disputant to emphasize the same goal. This might occur in cases such as a dispute over garden damage between two members of the same one-blood group who have a long history of neighborly relations. Here the goal is obviously some amount of financial restitution, but more important is maintaining an ongoing social relationship. The garden owner will ask for reasonable damages, and the pig owner will not refuse them. This is exactly what happened in the cases of the "hungry hog." It is not surprising that in the first case Sine and Koma privately negotiated an amicable agreement with Gui. To ask for an inappropriately large compensation payment or to refuse a reasonable request would needlessly jeopardize valuable relations.

A second, but very different, example of complementary situational criteria involves a dispute over land between persons who have had several previous altercations and who are members of different tribes that maintain a relationship of enmity. In this case I would predict coercion, constrained only by the potential threat of expansion into warfare. Despite the obvious difference in goals between this case and the previous one, in each the four criteria are complementary. Based on the nature of the grievance, the structural distance and the past histories, the disputants would have little difficulty setting a goal. In other words, trying to prioritize the criteria would cause little internal turmoil.

It is more common, however, for at least one of the situational criteria to suggest an emphasis on a goal different from or diametrically opposed to that suggested by another criteria. Take, for example, a case where a man commits adultery with the wife of a member of his own one-blood group. The nature of the grievance suggests a need for the husband to regain prestige through receiving a large compensation payment. At the same time, being members of the same group suggests a need to maintain harmonious relations. In such cases, setting goals is more difficult for the individual, as he or she must carefully weigh the various opposing factors before making decisions and taking actions.

COMPROMISE AND RECONCILIATION

One of the major assumptions made by anthropologists interested in dispute processing is that in "face-to-face" communities all parties accept balance, reconciliation, and harmony as primary values and will thus be willing to compromise differences (Starr and Yngvesson 1975:554). This view is held by major thinkers such as Gluckman (1955), Gulliver (1963), and Nader (1969a). When Starr and Yngvesson reanalyzed Gluckman's case materials they found that these ideals are frequently not manifest in behavior. This led them to ask, "What might concepts such as compromise and zero-sum mean, as *descriptions of outcomes,* when the goals of disputants are taken into account" (Starr and Yngvesson 1975:562).

As I have suggested, outcomes, in terms of cash payments, may often be best viewed as a *means* of obtaining more basic underlying goals, particularly when the relations between the disputants are multiplex or highly valued. Moreover, I argue that there is no automatic congruence between the desire for reconciliation and the observable outcome of compromise. To the contrary, I suggest that various cultural factors at work in Simbu society are antithetical to the notion that reconciliation is achieved primarily through compromise.

T. E. Barnett (1972:64) reports that "The Melanisian view about compensation for injury caused to a person or property is far more like one of absolute liability than liability based on fault. It does not seem to matter whether a person injured a victim deliberately, negligently or through no fault of his own. The person injured must be compensated anyway." This generalization holds true in Mul, and, as a result, the notion of fault cannot be used as a point of argument from which to effect a compromise (see Podolefsky 1982). Informants state that, in the past, groups compensated others for deaths incurred during warfare through large gifts and not through *negotiated* compensation payments. The gift was certainly a payment, albeit not negotiated. An insufficient payment led to renewed fighting, whereas a generous payment ended overt hostilities.

We saw that in case thirteen an extremely large compensation was given by Hui Kora to his wife's father after his action of burning his wife's house had threatened the life of his wife's brother. Making a payment that was substantially larger than expected served to restore a valuable social relationship as well as restore prestige to both parties. It is likely that bargaining or attempting to negotiate a compromise would have failed to reestablish the highly valued relations between Hui and his wife's father.

CONCLUSION

I came to the New Guinea Highlands to learn how people in acephelous societies lacking indigenous systems of courts and corrections deal with trouble cases through either traditional means or the imposed, colonial legal system. How do they attempt to resolve conflicts between strangers or between kin and neighbors? In trying to communicate to you some of what I have learned, I set the stage by describing those aspects of Simbu society most relevant to the analysis of conflict. I then examined what I have called the structure of opportunity, providing some insight into litigants' options in conflict situations. Finally, I looked at the individuals' behaviors within the contextual constraints of socially approved options and the norms and values of society.

Throughout this book I have been concerned with how and why individuals make particular choices during dispute processing. In focusing on the disputants' options, I turned to an antecedent analytic unit, the grievance situation, to provide the criteria used by Simbu to make decisions that lead to observable actions and behaviors. As such, my analysis has remained sociological rather than psychological. I have not been concerned with the cognitive aspects of the decision-making process.

My focus has been on the individual and his or her options. I view the statistical pattern that results from the use of various modes of dispute handling as the end result of a series of individual choices. My analysis of sixty-five observed dispute cases and hundreds of pages of interview and observational data suggest that there are four primary criteria that influence disputants' choices, which, in turn, lead to this observable pattern, or case load distribution. The four criteria are: the nature of the grievance, the structural relations between disputants, the history of relations between the individual disputants, and the history of relations between their social groups. The latter three of these criteria are the social context of the dispute.

In this final chapter, I have relied on the data presented throughout to elaborate on the causal relationship between the grievance situation and decisions and actions. Viewing the interplay of the structural and situational criteria and the concomitant complementarity or opposition of goals in this fashion allows for a large degree of variation in human behavior and provides insight into why discussions of dispute behavior in face-to-face communities cannot be understood by reference to stated norms regarding dispute processing. Moreover, I suggest that this variation is normal and necessary in the handling of disputes in small-scale face-to-face communities where social relations are necessarily multiplex, ongoing, and highly valued.

References

Abel, R.
1969. Customary Laws of Wrongs in Kenya: An Essay in Research Method. *American Journal of Comparative Law* 17:573.

Abel, R.
1974. A Comparative Theory of Dispute Institutions in Society. *Law and Society Review* 88(2):217–349.

Aufenanger, H.
1959. The War-magic Houses in the Wahgi Valley and Adjacent Areas (N.G.). *Anthropos* 54:1–25.

Barnett, T. E.
1972a. Law and Justice Melanesian Style. In A. Clunies Ross and J. Langmore (eds.), *Alternative Strategies for Papua and New Guinea*. Melbourne: Melbourne University Press.

Barton, R. F.
1919. *Ifugao Law*. University of California Publications in American Archaeology and Ethnology, Vol. 15.

Barton, R. F.
1949. *The Kalingas*. Chicago: University of Chicago Press.

Bercovitch, J.
1984. *Social Conflicts and Third Parties*. Boulder, CO: Westview Press.

Bernard, H. R., P. Killworth, D. Kronenfeld, and L. Sailer.
1984. The Problem of Informant Accuracy: The Validity of Retrospective Data. *Annual Review of Anthropology* 13:495–517.

Berndt, R. M.
1962. *Excess and Restraint*. Chicago: University of Chicago Press.

Berndt, R. M.
1964. Warfare in the New Guinea Highlands. *American Anthropologist,* 66(4, pt. 2):183–203.

Berndt, R. M., and P. Lawrence (eds.).
1971. *Politics in New Guinea*. Nedlands: University of Western Australia Press.

Black, M., and D. Metzger.
1965. Ethnographic Description and the Study of Law. *American Anthropologist,* 69(6, pt. 2):141–165.

Bohannan, P.
1965. The Differing Realms of the Law. In L. Nader (ed.), *The Ethnography of Law. American Anthropologist,* 69(6, pt. 2).

Bowers, N.
1968. The Ascending Grassland. Unpublished Ph.D. thesis. New York: Columbia University.

Brandewie, E.
   1971. The Place of the Big Man in Traditional Hagen Society in the Central Highlands of New Guinea. *Ethnology* 10:194–210.

Brookfield, H. C.
   1973. Full Circle in Chimbu. In H. C. Brookfield (ed.), *The Pacific in Transition*. New York: St. Martins Press.

Brookfield, H. C., and P. Brown.
   1963. *Struggle for Land*. Melbourne: Oxford University Press.

Bromley, M.
   1960. A Preliminary Report on Law among the Grand Valley Dani of Netherlands New Guinea. *Nieuw-Guinea Studien, Jaarang* 4 Nr. 3, Juli:235–259.

Brown, P.
   1960. Chimbu Tribes: Political Organization in the Eastern Highlands of New Guinea. *Southwestern Journal of Anthropology* 16:22–35.

Brown, P.
   1961. Chimbu Death Payments. *Journal of the Royal Anthropological Institute* XCI: 77–96.

Brown, P.
   1962. Non-agnates among the Patrilineal Chimbu. *Journal of the Polynesian Society* 71:57–69.

Brown, P.
   1963a. From Anarchy to Satrapy. *American Anthropologist* 65:1–15.

Brown, P.
   1963b. Review of Berndt. *British Journal of Sociology* 14:292–293.

Brown, P.
   1964. Enemies and Affines. *Ethnology* 3:335–356.

Brown, P.
   1966a. Social Change and Social Movements. In E. K. Fisk (ed.), *New Guinea on the Threshold*. Canberra: Australian National University Press.

Brown, P.
   1966b. Goodby to All That? In E. H. Hipsey (ed.), *An Integrated Approach to Nutrition and Society: The case of the Chimbu*. New Guinea Research Bulletin 9:31–48.

Brown, P.
   1967. Chimbu Political System. *Anthropological Forum* 2(1):36–52.

Brown, P.
   1969. Marriage in Chimbu. In R. M. Glasse and M. J. Meggitt (eds.), *Pigs, Pearlshells and Women*. Englewood Cliffs, NJ: Prentice Hall.

Brown, P.
   1970a. Chimbu Transactions. *Man* 5:99–117.

Brown, P.
   1970b. *Mingge*-Money: Economic Change in the New Guinea Highlands. *Southwestern Journal of Anthropology* 26:242–259.

Brown, P.
   1972. *The Chimbu*. Cambridge: Shenkman.

Brown, P.
   1974. Mediator in Social Change: New Roles for Big-men. *Mankind* 9:224–230.

Brown, P.
1982a. Conflict in the New Guinea Highlands. *Journal of Conflict Resolution* 26:525–546.

Brown, P.
1982b. Chimbu Disorder: Tribal Fighting in Newly Independent Papua New Guinea. *Pacific Viewpoint* 22:1–21.

Brown, P., and H. C. Brookfield.
1959. Chimbu Land and Society. *Oceania* 30:1–75.

Brown, P., and H. C. Brookfield.
1967. Chimbu Settlement and Residence: A Study of Patterns, Trends, and Ideosyncracy. *Pacific Viewpoint* 8(2):119–51.

Brown, P., and A. Podolefsky.
1976. Population Density, Agricultural Intensity, Land Tenure and Group Size in the New Guinea Highlands. *Ethnology* 15(3):211–238.

Brown, P., and G. Winfield.
1965. Some Demographic Measures Applied to Chimbu Census and Field Data. *Oceana* 3(35):175–190.

Burridge, K. O. L.
1957. Disputing in Tangu. *American Anthropologist* 59:763–780.

Chowning, A.
1973. *An Introduction to the Peoples and Cultures of Melanesia*. Addison-Wesley Module No. 38.

Cohen, P.
1968. *Modern Social Theory*. New York: Basic Books.

Collier, J. F.
1973. *Social Control in Zanacanten*. Palo Alto, CA: Stanford University Press.

Collier, J. F.
1975. Legal Processes. In B. J. Siegal (ed.), *Annual Reviews of Anthropology* Vol. 4. Palo Alto, CA: Annual Reviews.

Colson, E.
1953. Social Control and Vengeance in Plateau Tonga Society. *Africa* 23:199–212.

Comaroff, J. L., and S. A. Roberts.
1977. The Invocation of Norms in Dispute Settlement: The Tswana Case. In I. Hamnett (ed.), *Social Anthropology and Law*. A. S. A. Monograph No. 14. New York: Academic Press.

Conklin, H. C.
1961. The Study of Shifting Cultivation. *Current Anthropology* 2:27–61.

Criper, C.
1968. The Politics of Exchange: A Study of Ceremonial Exchange among the Chimbu. Unpublished Ph.D. Thesis. Australian National University.

Day, A. T., and L. H. Day.
1973. Cross National Comparison and Population Density. *Science* 181:1016–1022.

Durkheim, E.
1893. *The Division of Labor in Society*. New York: Free Press (1933 edition).

DuToit, B. M.
1975. *Akuna: A New Guinea Village Community*. Rotterdam: A. A. Balkema.

130   REFERENCES

Epstein, A. L.
1967a. The Case Method in the Field of Law. In A. L. Epstein (ed.), *The Craft of Social Anthropology*. London: Travistock.

Epstein, A. L.
1967b. *The Craft of Social Anthropology*. London: Travistock.

Epstein, A. L.
1972. Indigenous Law. In *Encyclopedia of Papua New Guinea*. Melbourne: Melbourne University Press. pp. 631–634.

Epstein, A. L.
1973. Law. In I. Hogbin (ed.), *Anthropology in Papua New Guinea*. Melbourne: Melbourne University Press.

Epstein, A. L.
1974. Introduction. In A. L. Epstein (ed.), *Contention and Dispute*. Canberra: Australian National University Press.

Evans-Pritchard, E. E.
1937. *Witchcraft, Oracles, and Magic Among the Zande*. New York: Oxford University Press.

Evans-Pritchard, E. E.
1940. *The Nuer*. New York: Oxford University Press.

Felstiner, W.
1974. Influences of Social Organization on Dispute Processing. *Law and Society Review* 9(1):63–94.

Fisher, R., and W. Ury.
1981. *Getting to Yes*. New York: Penguin Books.

Flanagan, J.
1981. To Be the Same but Different: A Wovan Dilemma. In R. Gordon (ed.), *The Plight of Peripheral People in Papua New Guinea*. Peterborough, N.H.: Transcript Printing (for Cultural Survival).

Glaser, B.
1965. The Constant Comparative Method of Qualitative Analysis. *Social Problems* 12:436–445.

Glasse, R. M.
1959. Revenge and Redress among the Huli: A Preliminary Account. *Mankind* 5:273–289.

Glasse, R. M.
1965. The Huli of the Southern Highlands. In P. Lawrence and M. J. Meggitt (eds.), *Gods, Ghosts, and Men in Melanesia*. Melbourne: Oxford University Press.

Glasse, R. M.
1968. *Huli of Papua: A Cognatic Descent System*. Cahiers de l'Homme, n.s. VIII. Paris and The Hague: Mouton.

Glasse, R. M.
1969. Marriage in South Fore. In R. M. Glasse and M. J. Meggitt (eds.), *Pigs, Pearlshells and Women*. Englewood Cliffs, NJ: Prentice Hall.

Glasse, R. M. and S. Lindenbaum
1971. South Fore Politics. In R. M. Bernt and P. Lawrence (eds.), *Politics in Papua New Guinea*. Nedlands: University of Western Australia Press.

Gluckman, M.
1955. *The Judicial Process among the Barotse of Northern Rhodesia*. Manchester: Manchester University Press.

Gluckman, M.
1958. *Analysis of Social Situation in Modern Zululand*. Institute for Social Research, University of Zambia. Manchester University Press. (Originally in Bantu Studies: 1940.)

Gluckman, M.
1961. Ethnographic Data in British Social Anthropology. *Sociological Review* 9:5–17.

Godelier, M.
1982. Social Hierarchies Among the Baruya of New Guinea. In A. J. Strathern (ed.), *Inequality in New Guinea Highlands Societies*. Cambridge: Cambridge University Press.

Goldman, L.
1984. *Talk Never Dies: The Language of Huli Disputes*. New York: Travistock.

Gordon, R.
1983. The Decline of the Kiapdom and the Resurgence of "Tribal Fighting" in Enga. *Oceania* 53:205–223.

Greenhouse, C. J.
1985. Mediation: A Comparative Approach. *Man* (N.S.) 20:90–114.

Gulliver, P. H.
1963. *Social Control in an African Society*. London: Routledge and Kegan Paul.

Gulliver, P. H.
1969a. Introduction: Case Studies of Law in Non-Western Societies. In L. Nader (ed.), *Law in Culture and Society*. Chicago: Aldine.

Gulliver, P. H.
1969b. Dispute Settlement without Courts: The Ndendeuli of Southern Tanzania. In L. Nader (ed.), *Law in Culture and Society*. Chicago: Aldine.

Gulliver, P. H.
1971. *Neighbors and Networks*. Berkeley, CA: University of California Press.

Gulliver, P. H.
1973. Negotiation as a Mode of Dispute Settlement: Towards a General Model. *Law and Society Review* 7:667–691.

Gulliver, P. H.
1977. On Mediators. In I. Hamnett (ed.), *Social Anthropology and Law*. A. S. A. Monograph No. 14. New York: Academic Press.

Gulliver, P. H.
1979. *Disputes and Negotiations*. New York: Academic Press.

Hamnett, I. (ed.).
1977. *Social Anthropology and Law*. A. S. A. Monograph No. 14. New York: Academic Press.

Hatanaka, S.
1972. Leadership and Socio-economic Change in Sina Sina, New Guinea Highlands. Port Moresby and Canberra: New Guinea Research Bulletin No. 45.

Hatanaka, S.
1973. Conflict of Laws in a New Guinea Highlands Society. *Man* 8:59–73.

Hayano, D.
  1973. Sorcery Death, Proximity, and the Perception of Out Groups: The Tauna Awa of
        New Guinea, *Ethnology* 7(2):179–191.

Heider, K.
  1970. *The Dugum Dani,* Chicago: Aldine.

Heider, K.
  1972. The Dani of West Irian: An Ethnographic Companion to the Film *Dead Birds*.
        Warner Module No. 2.

Hemple, C. G.
  1952. *Fundamentals of Concept Formation in Empirical Science*. Chicago: Chicago
        University Press.

Hide, R. L.
  1971. *Land Demarkation and Disputes in the Chimbu District of the New Guinea High-
        lands*. New Guinea Research Bulletin No. 40. Canberra; Australian National
        University.

Hide, R. L.
  1973. *The Land Titles Commission in Chimbu: An Analysis of Colonial Land Law
        Practices*. New Guinea Research Bulletin No. 50. Canberra: Australian National
        University.

Hide, R. L.
  1974. On the Dynamics of Some New Guinea Highland Pig Cycles. Unpublished.

Hoebel, E. A.
  1942. Fundamental Legal Concepts in Primitive Law. *Yale Law Journal* 51:951–966.

Hoebel, E. A.
  1954. *The Law of Primitive Man*. Cambridge: Harvard University Press.

Hogbin, H. I., and C. H. Wedgwood.
  1953. Local Grouping in Melanesia. *Oceania* 23:241–246 and 24:58–76.

Howlett, D., R. Hide, and E. Young, with J. Arba, H. Bi, and B. Kaman.
  1976. *Chimbu: Issues in Development*. Development Studies Centre Monograph No. 4.
        Canberra: Australian National University Press.

Johnson, S. H.
  1969. Criminal Law and Punishment. In B. J. Brown (ed.), *Fashion of Law in New
        Guinea*. Sydney: Butterworths.

Kambu, J., J. Lagogo, J. Dawekai, and K. Townadong.
  1974. Report on University of Papua New Guinea Chimbu Students' Investigation of a
        Reported Crisis in Chimbu Schools. Chimbu Students Association. University of
        Papua New Guinea, Port Morsby, Mimeo.

Kelly, R. C.
  1976. Witchcraft and Sexual Relations. In P. Brown and G. Buchbinder (eds.), *Man and
        Woman in the New Guinea Highlands*. Washington, DC: American Anthropologi-
        cal Association.

Kidder, R.
  1983. *Connecting Law and Society*. Englewood Cliffs, NJ: Prentice Hall.

Koch, K. F.
  1970. Warfare and Anthrophagy in Jale Society. *Bijdragen tot de Taal-, Land-en Volken-
        kunde* 126:37–58.

Koch, K. F.
  1974b. *War and Peace in Jalimo*. Cambridge: Harvard University Press.

Langness, L. L.
  1964a. Bena Bena Social Structure. Unpublished Ph.D. Thesis. Seattle: University of
    Washington.

Langness, L. L.
  1964b. Some Problems in the Conceptualization of Highlands Social Structures. *American
    Anthropologist* 66 (4, pt. 2):162–182.

Langness, L. L.
  1968. Bena Bena Political Ogranization. *Anthropological Forum* 2:180–198.

Lawrence, P. and M. J. Meggitt (eds.).
  1965. *Gods, Ghosts and Men in Melanesia*. Melbourne: Oxford University Press.

Leahy, M. J.
  1934. Never Before Seen By White Men: Cannibals' Villages in New Guinea. London:
    The London Illustrated News, December 29, pp. 1090–1091.

Leahy, M. J., and M. Crain.
  1937. *The Land That Time Forgot*. London: Hunt and Blackett.

Lindenbaum, S.
  1971. Sorcery and Structure in Fore Society. *Oceania* 41:277–287.

Lindenbaum, S.
  1972. Sorcerers, Ghosts, and Polluting Women: An Analysis of Religious Belief and
    Population Control. *Ethnology* 11:241–253.

Lindenbaum, S.
  1979. *Kuru Sorcery*. Palo Alto, CA: Mayfield.

Lindenbaum, S., and R. M. Glasse.
  1969. Fore Age Mates. *Oceania* 34(3):165–173.

Llewelyn, K. N., and E. A. Hoebel.
  1941. *The Cheyenne Way*. Norman: University of Oklahoma Press.

Lowman-Vayda, C.
  1968. Maring Big Men. *Anthropological Forum* 2:199–243.

Malinowski, B.
  1913. *The Family among the Australian Aboriginies*. London: University of London Press.

Malinowski, B.
  1915. The Natives of Mailu: Preliminary Results of the Robert Mond Research Work in
    British New Guinea. Transactions of the Proceedings of the Royal Society of South
    Australia 34:494–706.

Malinowski, B.
  1926. *Crime and Custom in a Savage Society*. London: Kegan Paul, Trench, Trubnery,
    and Co.

Malinowski, B.
  1934. Introduction. In I. Hogbin (ed.), *Law and Order in Polynesia*. New York: Shoe
    String Press.

Mayhew, B., R. Levinger, J. McPherson, and T. James.
  1972. System Size and Structural Differentiation in Formal Organizations. *American
    Sociological Review* 37:629–633.

Meggitt, M.
　1957. Mae Enga Political Organization. *Mankind* 5:133–137

Meggitt, M.
　1958. The Enga of the New Guinea Highlands. *Oceania* 28:253–330.

Meggitt, M.
　1965. *The Lineage System of the Mae Enga*. Edinburgh: Oliver and Boyd.

Meggitt, M.
　1969. Introduction. In R. M. Glasse and M. Meggitt (eds.), *Pigs, Pearlshells and Women*. Englewood Cliffs NJ: Prentice Hall.

Meggitt, M.
　1977. *Blood is their Argument: Warfare Among the Mae Enga Tribesmen of the New Guinea Highlands*. Palo Alto CA: Mayfield.

Merry, S.
　1982. The Social Organization of Mediation in Non-industrial Societies. In. R. Abel (ed.), *The Politics of Justice*. New York: Academic Press.

Michalowski, R. J.
　1985. *Order, Law, and Crime*. New York: Random House.

Modjeska, N.
　1982. Production and Inequality: Perspectives from Central New Guinea. In A. J. Strathern (ed.), *Inequality in New Guinea Highlands Societies*. Cambridge: Cambridge University Press.

Moore, S. F.
　1970. Law and Anthropology. In B. J. Siegel (ed.), *Biennial Review of Anthropology*. Stanford: Stanford University Press.

Moore, S. F.
　1972. Legal Liability and Evolutionary Interpretation: Some Aspects of Strict Liability, Self-help, and Collective Responsibility. In M. Gluckman (ed.), *The Allocation of Responsibility*. Manchester: Manchester University Press.

Nader, L.
　1965a. The Anthropological Study of Law. *American Anthropologist* 67(6):3–32.

Nader, L.
　1965b. The Ethnography of Law. *American Anthropologist* (special edition) 67(6) pt. 2.

Nader, L.
　1969a. Styles of Court Procedure: To Make the Balance. In L. Nader (ed.), *Law in Culture and Society*. Chicago: Aldine.

Nader, L.
　1969b. *Law in Culture and Society*. Chicago: Aldine.

Nader, L. and B. Yngvesson
　1973. On Studying the Ethnography of Law and Its Consequences. In J. J. Honigmann (ed.), *Handbook of Social and Cultural Anthropology*. Chicago: Rand McNally and Co.

Newman, K. S.
　1983. *Law and Economic Organization: A Comparative Study of Preindustrial Societies*. New York: Cambridge University Press.

Newman. P. L.
　1965. *Knowing the Gururumba*. New York: Holt, Rinehart and Winston.

Nilles, J.
  1950. The Kuman of the Chimbu Region, Central Highlands, New Guinea. *Oceania* 21:25–65.
Nilles, J.
  1953. The Kuman People: A Study of Cultural Change in a Primitive Society in the Central Highlands of New Guinea. *Oceania* 24:1–27 and 119–131.
Notes and Queries on Anthropology.
  1951. Royal Anthropological Institute of Great Britain and Ireland.
O'Brien, D.
  1969. Marriage among the Konda Valley Dani. In R. M. Glasse and M. J. Meggitt (eds.), *Pigs, Pearshells and Women.* Englewood Cliff NJ: Prentice Hall.
O'Brien, D. and A. Ploeg.
  1964. Acculturation Movements among the Western Dani. In R. M. Berndt (ed.), *American Anthropologist,* 66(4 pt. 2) 281–292.
Paney, P., T. Barnett, W. Tiden, W. Bai, and J. Nombri.
  1973. Report of the Committee Investigating Tribal Fighting in the Highlands. Port Moresby.
Papua New Guinea Village Directory.
  1973. Papua New Guinea.
Pelto, P.
  1970. *Anthropological Research: the Structure of Inquiry.* New York: Harper and Row.
Peters, E. L.
  1967. Some Structural Aspects of the Feud among the Camel-herding Bedouin of Cyrenaica. *Africa* (37)3:261–282.
Peters, H. L.
  1975. Some Chapters from Dani Religious Life. Irian: Bulletin of Irian Jaya Development 4(2):1–99.
Phillips, B. S.
  1971. *Social Research: Strategy and Tactics.* New York: MacMillan.
Ploeg, A.
  1966. Some Comparative Remarks about the Dani of the Balim Valley and the Dani of Bokondini. *Bijdragen tot de Tall-, Land-en Volkenkunde* 122.2:254–273
Podolefsky, A. M.
  1978. Pattern, Process and Decision Making in New Guinea Highlands Dispute Handling. Unpublished Ph.D. Thesis. SUNY at Stony Brook.
Podolefsky, A. M.
  1982. To Make the Belly Cold: Conceptions of Justice in the New Guinea Highlands. Paper presented at the annual meeting of the American Anthropological Association.
Podolefsky, A. M.
  1983. *Case Studies in Community Crime Prevention.* Springfield, IL: Charles C. Thomas, Publisher.
Podolefsky, A. M.
  1984. Contemporary Warfare in the New Guinea Highlands. *Ethnology* 23(2):73–87.
Podolefsky, A. M.
  1987. Population Density, Land Tenure and Law in the New Guinea Highlands: Reflection on Legal Evolution. *American Anthropoligist,* 89(3):581–595.

Podolefsky, A., and F. DuBow.
  1981. *Strategies for Community Crime Prevention*. Springfield, IL: Charles C. Thomas, Publisher.

Pospisil, L.
  1958. *Kapauku Papuans and their Law*. New Haven, CT: Yale University Publications in Anthropology No. 54.

Pospisil, L.
  1963. *The Kapauku Papuans of West New Guinea*. New York: Holt, Rinehart and Winston.

Pospisil, L.
  1971. *Anthropology of Law: A Comparative Theory*. New Haven: Yale University Press.

Radcliffe-Brown, A. R.
  1933. Primitive Law. In *Encyclopaedia of the Social Sciences* 9:202–206.

Rappaport, R.
  1968. *Pigs for the Ancestors: Ritual in the Ecology of a New Guinea People*. New Haven, CT: Yale University Press.

Read, K. E.
  1965. *The High Valley*. New York: Scribners.

Reay, M.
  1959. *The Kuma*. Melbourne: Melbourne University Press.

Reay, M.
  1974. Changing Conventions of Dispute Settlement in the Minj Area. In A. L. Epstein (ed.), *Contention and Dispute*. Canberra: Australian National University Press.

Reay, M.
  1976. The Politics of a Witch Killing. *Oceania* 47:1–20.

Robbins, S. G.
  1970. Warfare, Marriage, and the Distribution of Goods in Auyana. Unpublished Ph.D. Thesis. Seattle: University of Washington.

Robinson, W. S.
  1950. Ecological Correlations and the Behavior of Individuals. *American Sociological Review* 15:351–357.

Roberts, S.
  1983. Mediation in Family Disputes. *Modern Law Review*. 46:537–557.

Rousseau, J.
  1754. *A Discourse on the Origin of Inequality*.

Sahlins, M.
  1963. Poor Man, Rich Man, Big Man, Chief: Political Types in Melanesia and Polynesia. *Comparative Studies in Society and History* 5(3):285–303.

Salisbury, R.
  1962. *From Stone to Steel*. London and New York: Cambridge.

Salisbury, R.
  1964. Despotism and the Australian Administration. *American Anthropolgist* 66(4):227–228.

Salisbury, R.
  1965. The Siane of the Eastern Highlands. In P. Lawrence and M. J. Meggitt (eds.), *Gods, Ghosts and Men in Melanesia*. Melbourne: Oxford University Press.

Scaglion, R.
1981. Samukundi Abalam Conflict Management: Implications for Legal Planning in Papua New Guinea. *Oceania* 22:28–38.

Scaglion, R.
1983. Introduction. In R. Scaglion (ed.), *Customary Law in Papua New Guinea*. Law Reform Commission Monograph No. 2. Port Moresby: Government Printing Office.

Scaglion, R.
1985. Kiaps as Kings: Abelam Legal Change in Historical Perspective. In D. Gewertz and E. Schieffelin (eds.), *History and Ethnohistory in Papua New Guinea*. Oceania Monograph No. 28. Sydney: University of Sydney.

Schafer, A.
1938. Im Wagital, dem paradies von Neuginea. *Steyler Missionsbote* 66(2):29–33, 75–79.

Schwartz, R. D.
1964. Social Factors in the Development of Legal Control: A Case Study of Two Israeli Settlements. *Yale Law Journal* 63:471–491.

Schwartz, R. D., and J. C. Miller.
1974. Legal Evolution and Societal Complexity. *American Journal of Sociology* 70:159–159.

Simmel, G.
1893. *Conflict and the Web of Group Affiliations*. New York: Free Press (1955).

Smith, R.
1975. Chumbu Population Density Study. Central Planning Office, Mt. Hagen.

Standish, B.
1974. The Highlands, *New Guinea* 8(3):4–30.

Starr, J.
1978a. *Dispute Settlement in Rural Turkey: an Ethnography of Law*. Leiden, Holland: E. J. Brill.

Starr, J.
1978b. Negotiations: A Pre-law Stage in Rural Turkish Disputes. In P. H. Gulliver (ed.), *Essays in Honor of Max Gluckman*. Leiden, Holland: E. J. Brill.

Starr, J.
1978c. Turkish Village Disputing Behavior. In L. Nader and H. Todd (eds.), *Disputing in Ten Societies*. New York: Columbia University Press.

Starr, J. and J. Pool.
1974. The Impact of a Legal Revolution in Rural Turkey. *Law and Society Review* 8(4, summer):533–560

Starr, J., and B. Yngvesson.
1975. Scarcity and Disputing: Zeroing-in on Compromise Decisions. *American Ethnologist* 2(3):553–566.

Sterling, M. W.
1943. The Native Peoples of New Guinea. Smithsonian Institution War Background Studies No. 9.

Strathern, A. J.
1966. Despots and Directors in the New Guinea Highlands. *Man* 1:356–367. (new series).

Strathern, A. J.
  1972. Political Development and Problems and Social Control in Mount Hagen. Sixth
    Waigani Seminar.

Strathern, A. J.
  1974. When Dispute Procedures Fail. In A. L. Epstein (ed.), *Contention and Dispute.*
    Canberra: Australia National University.

Strathern, M.
  1972a. Official and Unofficial Courts: Legal Assumptions and Expectations in a Highlands
    Community. New Guinea Research Bulletin No. 47. Canberra: Australian National
    University.

Strathern, M.
  1972b. Legality or Legitimacy: Hagener's Perception of the Judicial System. *Melanesian
    Law Journal*:5–27.

Turner, V. W.
  1957. *Schism and Continuity in an African Society.* Manchester: Manchester University
    Press.

Van Velson, J.
  1967. The Extended-case Method and Situational Analysis. In A. L. Epstein (ed.), *The
    Craft of Social Anthropology.* London: Travistock.

Vayda, A.
  1968. *Peoples and Cultures of the Pacific.* Garden City, NY: Natural History Press.

Village Directory.
  Papua New Guinea. 1973.

Wagner, R.
  1967. *The Curse of Souw.* Chicago: University of Chicago Press.

Wagner, R.
  1971. When a Chimbu Meets a Karimui. *New Guinea* 6(2):27–31.

Warren, N.
  1976. The Introduction of a Village Court. Iaser Discussion Paper No. 2, Institute of
    Applied Social and Economic Research. Papua New Guinea.

Westermark, G.
  1978. Village Courts in Question: The Nature of Court Procedure. *Melanesian Law
    Journal* 6:70–96.

Westermark, G.
  1981. Legal Pluralism and the Village Courts in Agarabi. Ph.D. Thesis, University of
    Washington.

Westermark, G.
  1983. Contemporary Intergroup Conflict in the Papua New Guinea Eastern Highlands.
    Paper presented at the Annual Meeting of the American Anthropological Associa-
    tion. Chicago, IL.

Wormsley, W.
  1982. Tribal Fighting, Law and Order, and Socioeconomic Development in Enga, Papua
    New Guinea. Paper presented at the meetings of the American Anthropological
    Association. Washington, D.C.

Wurm, S. A.
  1975. Eastern Central Trans-New Guinea Phylum Languages. In S. A. Wurm (ed.), *New*

Guinea Area Language and language Study, vol. 1. Papuan Languages and the New Guinea Language Scene. Pacific Linguistic Series C, No. 38, Department of Linguistics. Canberra: Australian National University.

Yngvesson, B.
   1976. Responses to Grievance Behavior: Extended Cases in a Fishing Community. *American Ethnologist* 3(2):353–373.

Young, M. W.
   1971. *Fighting with Food.* Cambridge: Cambridge University Press.

Young, M. W.
   1974. Private Sanctions and Public Ideology: Some Aspects of Self-help in Kalauna, Goodenough Island. In A. L. Epstein (ed.), *Contention and Dispute.* Melbourne: Oxford University Press.

Index